IN MEMORY OF
Philip Sherrard
a great teacher of Orthodoxy.

May your memory be eternal

In *Letters to Father Aristotle,* topics covered range from . . . *The
fundamental difference between the Orthodox East and Western
Christianity* — *The real reason so many second generation ethnic
Orthodox have left the Church* — *The great danger facing the
Church because of the secular climate in which the Church operates
in America* — *The problem of mixing politics and Orthodox faith* —
The problem of new modern translations of the Liturgy — *The challenges facing converts to Orthodoxy* — *The way to bring the
Orthodox prodigals back into the Church* — *The question of ecu-
menism and union with the Roman Catholic Church* — *and much,
much more.*

About the Author

Frank Schaeffer is a well-known author, movie director, and lec-
turer. Frank's writing has received widespread critical acclaim in
many newspapers and journals, including *The Los Angeles Times,
The Boston Globe, The Washington Post, Publishers Weekly, The
Orthodox Observer, The Word,* and *First Things.* Frank has directed many films, most recently a comedy for ABC television.
Frank is the author of a number of best-selling fiction and non-fic-
tion books, including *Portofino, Addicted to Mediocrity, A Time for
Anger,* and *Dancing Alone (The Quest for Orthodox Faith in the
Age of False Religion).* He is also the editor of *The Christian
Activist* newspaper, a leading journal of Orthodox opinion. Frank
serves on the parish council of the Greek Orthodox Church of
the Annunciation in Newburyport, Massachusetts. He is married
and has three children and two grandchildren.

About the Cover Art

The publishers and the author are indebted to the internationally
acclaimed American artist, Steven Hawley, for allowing his painting, "Hands of Man, Face of God" (© 1991) to be used on the
cover of this book. This work of art perfectly symbolizes the
warning set forth in *Letters to Father Aristotle.* The painting
depicts the hands and vestments of a Roman Catholic pope
serenely folded above a fragment of a Byzantine Orthodox icon of
Christ. It is as if Western Christianity has vanquished, absorbed,
or triumphed over the ancient Orthodox Church. All that remains
is a memory, a fragment of the past.

i

TABLE OF CONTENTS

Forwards to *Letters to Father Aristotle*
Introduction and Acknowledgments

world—The reason we were created—The one and only task of the
Orthodox Christian.

How the Orthodox lost their children to the secular world—Why
Orthodox young people abandon their faith—The anti-ascetic Western attitudes that destroy Orthodox faith—The fundamental misunderstanding of
America by the Orthodox and what it cost the Church—The desire to
"make it" in America and what it has cost the Orthodox—Orthodoxy vs.
"pluralism"—The corruption caused by ecumenism— The evangelistic
silence of the Orthodox.

The true nature of American culture—The culture of secularism exam-
ined—What American secularism and materialism has done to the
Orthodox Church—The "persecution" of seduction—What the Orthodox
ethnic emigrants really found in America.

The responsibility of those who leave the Orthodox Church for the secular
world—The mistake of thinking we Orthodox can become Protestants and
still be Christians—The lapsed Orthodox and how to get them back into
the Church—Disneyland vs. Athos—The need for monastic role models.

The solution to bringing the Orthodox prodigals back to the faith—How to
revitalize the Orthodox Church in the West—The need for holiness and
monasticism—The miracle achieved by the ethnic Orthodox who established the Orthodox Church in North America—The future of Orthodoxy:
What do we do now?—The role of confession, prayer, and fasting—The
loss of the sense of the sacred and the gospel of Jesus Christ: the "Pearl of
Great Price."

Orthodoxy is not to be studied, but lived—The difference between the
Western and Eastern view of Truth—The Orthodox distrust of dogma.

The mistaken premise of the secular environmental movement—The
Orthodox view of nature—Ethics in a morally silent universe.

feminism—Bishop Ware opens the door to the ordination of women—The new pan-Orthodox translation of the liturgy sponsored by SCOBA opens the door to liturgical innovation and reform in the name of modern translation.

What are "minor" and "major" issues in Church life?—What is truly important in spiritual life?—How a tiny wound can infect the whole body of Orthodoxy—The importance of environment and context—The era of a war on all tradition—Only the Church is perpetual; all else will disappear.

Why we Americans tolerate abortion—A society dedicated to "having a nice day"—The ultimate hedonistic culture—How can abortion be bad since so many "nice people" do it?—Hitler loved his dog Blondie, and we love babies.

The question of an Orthodox union with the Roman Catholic Church— The three insurmountable problems that must prevent this—The true state of the present Roman church—The post-Vatican II Roman Church is in chaos—The Pope presides over many "churches," not just one church— Orthodox liturgical purity vs. Roman liturgical chaos—Unity with diversity is the Orthodox way—How the world is unconsciously beginning to imitate the Orthodox idea of conciliarity —The worldwide trend toward local autonomy—How the Orthodox ecumenists are out of step with world history—The Pope as the new media Napoleon—The strange new Orthodox fascination with "unity" and humanistic ecumenical utopia.

How to work with non-Orthodox Christians—The true unity of shared purpose and belief—Where there is true common ground with Protestants and Roman Catholics—Unity through evangelism—The real way to become one with other Christians.

Spiritual self-discipline, the firebreak principle—Learning the habits of discipline—How to protect ourselves from the spirit of the world —Headcoverings and the loss of our "small" Orthodox traditions—Creating the atmosphere in

which divinization is possible —The road to barbarism is paved with incivility—
The details make us who we are—What will slowly destroy the Orthodox
Church—How the principle of marriage and childraising applies to the Church.

Other Books By Frank Schaeffer:

Portofino: A Novel

Dancing Alone (The Quest for Orthodox Faith in the Age of False Religion).

These and other titles are available from **Regina Press**. Call Toll Free (800) 636-2470

Forwards to
LETTERS TO FATHER ARISTOTLE

The function of the prophet of the Old Testament was twofold: to foretell the future, the coming of the Messiah, and the fulfillment of the vocation of the Hebrew people; and to declare to those people the will of God for them, to warn them of the danger of misunderstanding and distorting their vocation as a people, as well as to call them to account for their sins and disobedience and for their departures from God's righteousness. The prophets called them to repentance for their transgressions, chief among which was that of being influenced by the idolatrous and barbarous religions of their neighbors and adopting their ways.

Our Lord Jesus Christ Himself, in His own prophetic ministry, condemned false religion and false thinking about religion, and, in so doing, He deeply offended the self-righteous religious leaders who were responsible for guiding the people of Israel.

Throughout Her history the Church has been beset by the assaults of the Evil One: whether heresies that would undermine the doctrine of the Person of the Lord Himself (Arianism, Nestorianism, Monophysitism, etc.), or pressures for conformity (iconoclasm) and politically motivated alliances (the false union of Florence). Many Christians, at times a majority of them, were attracted by these destructive movements, and were offended at the prophetic voice, which was never lacking, that perceived the real dangers in them. The Church, by God's grace, overcame them all and reached the twentieth century intact.

It is my opinion that many Orthodox Christians today are willing for the Church to surrender to the temptation to conform to the role that contemporary society assigns to religion: to bless this world's so-called progress in the moral and spiritual spheres, to reject all exclusivity or uniqueness in the interest of unity, and to concern itself with the world of the here-and-now rather than with the world to come. Many are unaware of the primary danger that the Church faces: the gradual infiltration of materialistic, humanistic, and secularist thinking—that the ground is being laid for a Western captivity far worse than those of the past latinizations and protestantizations.

Forwards

Prophetic voices are needed to call us all back to the realization that the forces of this world still want to destroy the Church and the precious Truth that has been entrusted to Her—to understand that what the Church has is essential for the life of the world and its salvation and that this cannot be mitigated. These voices will offend—so be it!

One such voice is that of the author of *Letters to Father Aristotle*. Frank Schaeffer has come to us from where that secularism has already done a great deal of its damage, and he is in a unique position to discern the signs of the times. He is an intensely loyal Orthodox layman, loyal also to his local church and the jurisdiction to which it belongs. He is one of us, and we American Orthodox should give heed to what he has to say.

☨ **Bishop DMITRI**
Archbishop of Dallas (OCA)
August 9, 1995

Though addressed to a fictional priest, *Letters to Father Artistotle* could be—should be—and, in fact, is —addressed to me and to every Orthodox believer. This collection of letters is a call to "wake up and smell the incense"—to shake off our lethargy and face the positive and negative realities of our late twentieth-century world which subtly—and on occasion, not so subtly—are impacting the Church. These letters demand a response from me and from all of us, for common courtesy alsone requires that we each promptly and thoughtfully answer our mail. "Dear Frank . . ."

☨ **Bishop BASIL**
Anthiochian Orthodox Archdiocese of America
October 7, 1995

"Frank Schaeffer will surprise many cradle Greek Orthodox Christians with this book. One would think that he has lived as a Greek Orthodox all of his life, as he correctly describes the thinking of the Greek-American in

Forwards

relationship to the Church. Both the cradle Orthodox and the recent convert will receive enlightenment and a clear understanding about Greek Orthodox parish life. In regard to the cultural side of the parish, Schaeffer greatly assists the reader to a deeper understanding.

He correctly cautions about the bad and even heretical English translations which are used in some of our parishes, and the danger of evolving Roman Catholic and Protestant ideas which want to find their way into the life of the Church.

This book is really a guide to "common sense" Orthodoxy, which speaks of the need of an enhanced daily lifestyle of Orthodox Christians on practical matters, as well as theological imperatives.

He is deliberate in describing how the Orthodox Christian should be more concerned and sensitive in his relationship with the Church. To some he may seem too blunt and almost impolite. Yet, in general, his style of writing is parallel to the style of Saint Mark and his Gospel—no frills, no extraneous niceties, just direct and forthright commentary.

Hopefully this book will mark the rise of Orthodox Christians becoming more serious with their faith and having a greater concern for their salvation, as well as signal the downfall of creeping secularism and heretical ideas which are attempting to make Greek Orthodoxy just one more "nice" religion in America.

If the reader believes in the one Church, which the Lord Jesus Christ established and which will remain until He returns, then the reader must read this book."

⳨ **Bishop ISAIAH**
Greek Orthodox Diocese of Denver
Denver, October 16, 1995

Forwards

"In his latest book Frank Schaeffer continues his personal journey in the Orthodox Christian Faith in a most unique manner. He addresses various issues of faith and tradition by answering questions posed to a 'Fr. Aristotle.' Frank's positions are certainly informative and, unquestionably, expressed in a strong language characteristic of a zealous style which is not universally appreciated. Regardless, this book is edifying, and I am happy to endorse it."

✠ **Bishop METHODIOS**
Greek Orthodox Diocese of Boston
Boston, October 18, 1995

Introduction and Acknowledgments

This collection of essays in the form of fictional letters is an incomplete and imperfect attempt of one private citizen of the Orthodox Church to add his voice to the ongoing debate that rages between the Church and the secularizing, desacralized spirit of this age. (The opinions expressed herein do not represent more than the opinion of this one individual.) It seems to me that today an important debate is not only being carried on outside the Orthodox Church but within its gates. It is for this reason that these imaginary letters are addressed to a priest. Some readers may consider my "tone" to lack the deference to which the calling and person of a priest, even a fictional one, is entitled. However, for the purpose of this book, I am speaking with a more casual tone than I would when addressing a real priest, let alone my own spiritual father. To me Father Aristotle represents an old friend with whom I can be perfectly candid.

The above notwithstanding, the events described herein are factual. With this in mind, it seems to me that it is from *within* that the greatest dangers and temptations beset the Orthodox Church. And it is *within* the Church that a firm line must be drawn against the sack of our ancient liturgical and mystical treasures by the spirit of the age, a spirit very different than the Holy Spirit, who guides the Church.

I would like to thank His Eminence, Archbishop Dmitri of Dallas (OCA), for all his encouragement and timely advice. I would also like to thank Archbishop Dmitri, His Grace, Bishop Isaiah, His Grace, Bishop Basil (Antiochian Archdiocese), and His Grace, Bishop Methodios for their generous endorsements of this book. Three other people were also very helpful in preparing this text: Brother Isaac (St. Michael's Skete, Cañones, New Mexico), Father Alexey Young (Denver, Colorado), and my editor, Will Anderson. I also wish to thank Father Patrick Henry Reardon for allowing me to use his excellent essay as the appendix of this book.

I would like to thank my wife, Genie, for all her hard work in doing the word processing for this book and for her loving encouragement and guidance in all things. Last but not least I am indebted to my friend, Steve

Introduction and Acknowledgments

Hawley, for allowing me to use his magnificent painting, "Hands of Man, Face of God," as the artwork on the cover of my book.

Frank Schaeffer
September 22, 1995
Salisbury, Massachusetts

LETTER I

Dear Fr. Aristotle,

You asked me about my experiences *vis-a-vis* my conversion to Orthodoxy. As you know, I was chrismated into the Greek Orthodox Church in December of 1990 in Newburyport, Massachusetts. At that time I knew very little, in a practical way, about the Orthodox Church. I had read quite a lot about the historic Church and about the Fathers. I had also read a number of patristic texts, particularly some of the ante-Nicene Fathers. However, none of this meant that I knew anything about being Orthodox or how to conduct myself in an Orthodox Church.

Besides Fr. Chris, my priest, several very kind Greek ladies, particularly, Stella, Thelma, and Mary, who were active in our parish, took me under their wings. I fondly remember Thelma, who is a wonderful woman in her seventies, teaching me how to make the Orthodox sign of the cross, how to light my candle, how to venerate the icons, and several prayers her mother had taught her. At that time she and her delightful sister, Mary, were teaching the same traditions to Mary's three-year-old granddaughter. I was invited by them to tag along, sit next to them, and learn right along with Mary's grandchild. Stella made me one of her own family, introduced me to everyone at church and saw to it that I was never alone. It was a wonderful experience, and only the first of many wherein the Greek Orthodox community reached out to me, my wife, and my three children and engulfed us in an embrace of Aegean warmth and hospitality.

Never have I felt so welcomed and loved as by the Orthodox. This sense of welcome has not only been in my home community but in the many other Greek, Antiochian, Russian, and Ukrainian Orthodox communities that I have had the privilege to visit.

I am not the only convert who has experienced a warm Orthodox welcome. Not long ago I was invited to speak at a Lenten retreat at the Greek Orthodox Church in Little Rock, Arkansas. It was the second time I had spoken there. The first time, several years before, a number of Protestants had attended my talk. As a result, they became interested in Orthodoxy.

LETTER I

One family in particular—a doctor, his wife, and five children—were intrigued because their eldest son, then attending an evangelical Protestant college in Chicago, had recently converted to Orthodoxy on his own. His parents and siblings came to my talk to find out about the "weird, new cult" their son had joined! Well, it seems that my lecture on my journey from evangelical Protestantism to Orthodoxy intrigued them. They left, determined to learn more. A year later, by God's grace, the entire family was preparing for chrismation.

The week before their chrismation, the father suddenly died of a heart attack. As I recall, the funeral was set for Thursday. The family's chrismation had been scheduled, weeks before, for the Sunday of that same week. Imagine the family's consternation! Their dilemma was multiplied by two unusual factors. The first was the fact that the fundamentalist Protestant parents of the doctor's wife had literally disowned her because of her pending conversion to Orthodoxy. So the newly widowed woman was facing her bereavement alone. The second problem was that the family's chrismation had not yet taken place. Thus the question of whether the father could have an Orthodox funeral arose.

The priest called his bishop to ask for permission to give the father a funeral in the Orthodox Church. The bishop said that in this highly unusual situation he would need to refer to the canons of the Church and consult several other bishops before giving a verdict on what was to be done.

Meanwhile, the family decided to go ahead with the scheduled chrismations of the wife and children, no matter what the bishop decided in regard to the funeral. At that point the wife's mother and father told her they would not attend her husband's funeral if it was held in an Orthodox Church!

The next day the bishop called and said that since the husband's intent to be chrismated had been clear, and since the Church honors *intent*, that the father "was chrismated in Heaven by Christ." The Orthodox funeral could proceed.

LETTER I

Now this family did not yet know anyone very well in the church. Imagine how lonely they felt since none of their relatives would come to the funeral! At the funeral the mother and children walked, alone, to the area at the front of the church reserved for family. Suddenly, out of the back of the church, a little, stooped, elderly Greek woman, dressed all in black, marched forward. She could hardly speak any English and had barely met the convert family. Leaning on her cane, she walked up to where the mother was sitting and sat down next to her. She then put her arm around the mother's shoulders and said, in broken English, *"I you mother now!"*

To me this story sums up the mystery and majesty of the Orthodox Church, the beauty of the Greek people, the purity of the Church, and the love I have for the Orthodox who adopted me. What an oasis of familial kinship is the Orthodox community in the barbaric, impersonal desert of American individualism! To find Orthodox churches that are ready to adopt we orphans of the Western cataclysm is a rare privilege indeed!

I know that not everyone's experience with the Orthodox Church has been as blessed as mine. This is of course inevitable. But what else except imperfection can we expect? The Church is pure, but not everyone in it is. However, how wonderful that so many Orthodox are living lives so full of grace and truth that they are willing to share their treasures with complete strangers like me!

I know that sometimes in my speaking and writing about Orthodoxy I am misunderstood. This is my fault for not communicating more clearly. Some people think that when I say that often we Orthodox seem to concentrate too much on our "social club" and "ethnic activities" that I am against such activities *per se* or against ethnic pride. Nothing could be further from the truth! I love the ethnic and social activities of the Greek Orthodox parish to which I belong. I believe they represent the indispensable bonds of true human community. As a parish council member, I delight to participate, in a practical way, in everything from our annual food festival to our "Taverna nights." (My specialty is organizing our

3

annual rummage sale!) The point I try to make in my speeches that sometimes is misunderstood is only that the *heart* of Orthodoxy must not become or be seen to be our social life. Rather, the heart of church life should be participation in the sacramental mysteries.

When ascetic struggle and sacramental participation go hand-in-hand with warmth, compassion, social activities (yes, including food festivals, bake sales, clergy-laity bashes, basketball leagues, and dances), then a wonderful thing happens—the social aspects of our church life become imbued with transcendent, sacramental light. When the hospitality of old-country village life is unleashed to warm our frozen, utilitarian, North American hearts, a wonderful spirit of Christian love is created. This is a great treasure.

When it comes to the appropriateness of our beloved social activities, it is all a question of priorities. For instance, there is nothing wrong with the coffee hour as long as it follows a Liturgy in which everyone has truly participated from the heart. A problem arises only when the coffee hour effectively becomes the "Liturgy," in that it is the only part of the service that everyone shows up for on time and stays to the end of! It is then that our social activities threaten to eclipse the heart of the Church's authentic life.

The essence of the Church's life is supposed to be communion with God. It seems to me that this communion gives beautiful meaning to communion with our fellow men in the coffee hour, food festivals, dances, and our other exuberant social activities. It is all a question of perspective, priorities, and proportion.

But shortcomings and occasional mixed-up priorities notwithstanding, I love to be entertained when I visit Orthodox communities! Greeks, Palestinians, Russians, Lebanese, Ukrainians, Arabs, Japanese, Ethiopians, and all the rest of the diverse ethnic Orthodox groups have a tremendous and ancient inheritance of hospitality and charity springing directly from Holy Tradition itself. Orthodox hospitality is greater than any I have ever known. (My wife teases me about how different my mood is when I return

LETTER I

from visiting an Orthodox community than it used to be when I would speak in Protestant circles. The Orthodox most assuredly know how to celebrate!)

We are never alone or cut off from the fullness of life in our Orthodox communities. Orthodoxy is very physical. It is celebratory. It is ebullient. We embrace; we kiss our priest's hand; we eat holy bread; we make prostrations; we make the sign of the cross; we drink coffee; we love a long, good dinner with plenty of wine (ouzo optional!); we fast and get hungry; drops of candle wax are splattered on our shoes and trousers; we are sprinkled with basil-scented holy water; we are anointed with oil; we are overpowered by incense; we kiss the relics of the Saints-in-Christ; we venerate icons; we argue reasonably (and unreasonably); and we know we are *alive*! In other words, Orthodoxy addresses the whole person, not just his reason, emotions, or theological doctrine. We Orthodox are allowed to be complete. We do not have to pretend that the life of the spirit is somehow separate from the rest of existence.

Thank God for the rich, New Testament, Greek-Mediterranean-Byzantine-African-Arab-Slavic-Palestinian inheritance! If I ever feel regret, it is for all the years I spent needlessly languishing in the ice box of original sin, Augustinian determinism, and guilt! What a tragedy to be shackled by Puritan suspicion and dislike of the physical world. What an escape I made from winter to summer, from a frosty Dutch February to a balmy Greek August. How I thank God that I was inexplicably drawn into the Orthodox Church by the Holy Spirit!

As ever,
Frank

LETTER II

Dear Fr. Aristotle,

Sometimes I receive letters from converts to Orthodoxy complaining about how "ethnic" or "foreign" the Orthodox Church in North America is. Occasionally converts complain because some or all of the liturgy is in Greek or Church Slavonic. Sometimes they even complain because the food or social habits and customs are "different!" Some converts seem to believe that ethnic activities of the social kind are a "proof" of spiritual deadness or nominalism. It seems to me that they are mistaken.

The Orthodox Church certainly has Her share of very real problems, but so often the Church's real problems are not the ones that converts are concerned about. This is understandable. The Western convert is used to a religion that is an intellectual exercise. To the Western convert, therefore, the idea that there are other ways to deepen one's faith besides Bible study, prayer meetings, and listening to sermons comes as a shock.

Often it seems that the comments of new converts reflect an incomplete understanding of what the Orthodox Church is in Her fullness. As the converts' enlightenment about Orthodoxy deepens, often superficial worries begin to evaporate. This is especially true when a convert takes the trouble to really enter into the life of the local Orthodox community on a day-to-day level of practical involvement.

The Church of the ages has such great depth that, little-by-little, the convert is led beyond the mundane aspects of church life into a deeper understanding of the mystery of the Faith. In a small and excruciatingly slow and imperfect way, this is happening to me. I find that I have only scratched the surface. There is much more to the Orthodox Church than I ever dreamed. There is always a deeper level of enlightenment to which to aspire. And I find that often activities that at first seemed to be superficial, merely social, or "unspiritual" in the life of the church indeed have a tremendous spiritual dimension that takes time to appreciate.

It seems that some of the letters I get from some disgruntled converts

LETTER II

perhaps express the sentiments of a narrow-minded Americanism. But provincial attitudes can be grown out of. Many converts like me have begun to see that it is the fact the Orthodox Church is *different* than the surrounding North American-Protestant-Humanist culture that is one of the most wonderful things about it. Often we converts discover that the ethnic social activities that we tend to look down on as "unspiritual" in fact have a lot to do with the full spiritual life for which we hunger.

I must say that I have developed a great appreciation for some of the very aspects of Orthodox life that, a few years ago, I would have described as barriers to a convert's full participation in the life of the Orthodox Church. In fact, I have learned to appreciate certain aspects of Orthodox social life that I would have hardly paid attention to in the past.

What a relief it is to find a place where one can hear languages other than vernacularized, mediocre, Americanized English spoken. How extraordinary to find an oasis of ancient civility and culture in the middle of the American "multicultural," "politically correct" wasteland in which everything has been homogenized and "Disneyfied" into one, long, seamless strip mall of putrid commercialism and moral equivalency. What a blessing to discover serious, awe-inspiring worship in the midst of the trivialized, user-friendly, undemanding entertainments that are passed off as "church" in both Roman Catholic and Protestant American society today. What a blessing to be made to work hard at my faith instead of being spoon-fed easy, prepackaged "spirituality" that always seems to appeal to the lowest common intellectual and esthetic denominator.

Certainly we Orthodox need to communicate the Truth in the language of the people. But I hope the growing need to teach in English in North America will not be at the expense of the priceless heritage of two thousand years of Orthodox history and culture in the Greek, Arab, Russian, African, and other diverse Orthodox communities. And I hope that the English used in our worship will be worthy of the poetic and literary beauty that is the iconic inheritance of the Orthodox.

LETTER II

What a short-sighted provincialism is at work when we converts want to "update" the Church, Protestantize—or worse, Americanize—the Orthodox treasures of the ages! How selfish of us to expect that the Church of the ages must change overnight to meet us rather than to work to change ourselves to meet the Church! How myopic of us it is if we do not take part in an authentic and historic culture when we live in a country that hardly has a history (let alone a cultural-religious identity) or a sacramental tradition of its own! How tragic it is that some people have such strong doubts about the Protestant or Roman Catholic American experience that they wish to convert to Orthodoxy, only to then try and change the Orthodox Church into a kind of "Orthodox," Americanized Protestantism!

Compassion demands that converts be welcomed. And usually we are. And compassion demands that there be teaching in the language of the people. And usually there is. But the baby must not be thrown out with the bathwater. The Church must not lose Her priceless, timeless character in order to suit American tastes as they spiral downward to a new low with each passing day.

We converts need to understand that we are not just "switching churches." We must understand that the Orthodox East is *fundamentally different* than the Latin West. This is something that I slowly, painfully, and imperfectly have been learning.

One of the major differences between Orthodox East and Latin West is that we of the Orthodox way do not look to reason and science as our primary source of Truth. We trust the uncreated light of Holy Mystery. We strive for union with God through ascetic struggle. We pray for a flood of Divine revelation and a genuine if incremental change of character. The Aristotelian-Augustinian-Scholastic-Protestant and "scientific" West, on the other hand, believes in reason and dogma as the means to the Truth if, that is, they believe in Truth at all.

We of the East believe that divinization is possible. We believe that the body and soul are one. We believe that the ascetic and monastic struggle to curb our passions is indispensable for salvation since salvation is a journey that must be completed in a rebirth that ends in divinization. These beliefs for the Orthodox Christian are not a matter of "a personal faith" but are the way of *being*. And this way of being is at odds with the West's faith in reason, dogma, and personal, subjective experience. The Orthodox way is not personalized or subjective, because it is communal. It is a shared way, a common way. It is a road of faith that has been worn smooth by countless feet.

All of the points mentioned above, and much more, create a completely different attitude on the part of the Orthodox toward life and the physical world than that of Western Christians. We may look at the same world, but we see different things. We may use the same words, but we hear different meanings.

Conversely, the other side of the coin of our Orthodox emphasis on ascetic struggle is the fact that without a tradition of fasting, feasting loses its meaning. Joy is the other side of struggle. The scholastic, rationalistic West has lost its Christian joy because it no longer has a place for the pain of the heart and the struggle of obedience to save the soul.

To the West, salvation is a matter of theology, dogma, personalized subjective experience, and rational thought. But for we who are struggling to become Christ through Christ's example, an ascetic journey is the only road to faith. This journey is not individualistic. We come to God as "we," not "I."

I believe that it is this unique awareness of the communal Orthodox approach to salvation that we must be careful not to lose and that the ethnic social fabric of the Orthodox Church is not incidental to it, but part of this communal journey of faith.

Because of this, we must not seek to replace the authentic ethnic social structures of the Orthodox community with the cold, sterile hypocrisy of

LETTER II

evangelical Protestant-style "friendliness," wherein everyone is "welcomed," then forgotten. We do not want to replace Orthodox joy with superficial American "fun," or unconditional familial loyalty with mere acquaintanceship.

It seems apparent that we Orthodox cannot have real friendship with God or man without real community. This is why the breakup of traditional, old-country village life was such a tragedy for those who immigrated to our rootless land. In this regard, converts or Westernized Orthodox who wish to make North American Orthodoxy less "ethnic" are being short-sighted. Some of the only authentic villages (in other words, tight-knit, stable communities) on North American soil are to be found in the ethnic Orthodox churches. These villages are a unique oasis of communion, responsibility, and family life in a very impersonal urban desert.

It seems to me that the authentic Orthodox village-church-community will not remain a community if it severs its ties with its ethnic past. It will become something else. New, stable, lasting ties that bind people together and make them truly care for one another are not going to be created overnight in our unstable, disintegrating, so-called "upwardly mobile" society. Indeed, new Orthodox convert churches filled with Americanized individualists would themselves do well to adopt a greater "ethnic style" of practical, village social life if they wish to survive and grow. The spiritual ties that bind cannot be created by wishing for them. It seems that spiritual community must be created within a living, physical community. From the Acts of the Apostles to our own day, we see the Christian community is not an idea; it is a practical reality or nothing at all.

We converts cannot have our cake and eat it too. If we love the treasures of the Orthodox Church, we had better pause to reflect on just why, in human terms, these treasures have been preserved intact for two thousand years.

It is no coincidence that the Truth has been preserved in tightly knit nation-clans. (This is nothing new. It began with the Israelites' twelve

LETTER II

tribes, and the life of the early Church was nothing if not communal.) And it is no coincidence that these nation-clans—these "villages"—revolve around family life, monastic life, the Church's calendar of feasting and fasting, social activities, and the ancient languages of the historic Christian faith.

It is not mere happenstance that our Orthodox communities have many practical social activities that draw people into deep and lasting friendships. Bake sales, lamb roasts, Taverna nights, basketball leagues, and dances are sacred activities when they draw like-minded people together in the context of the local church. This is especially so if the participants in these activities, their children, and their children's children reject the pyrrhic "upward mobility" of American life and stay in one place long enough to provide a truly stable environment. It is only possible to have a community if its members are more committed to *it* than to their careers. Only when people stay in one place can they exercise the unconditional love that is the prerequisite to love of neighbor.

The person you bake bread with year after year for the church's food festival will pray for your soul when you die. Moreover, he or she will look after the spiritual and physical welfare of your children and your children's children. The bread you bake together, the lamb you roast, the raffle tickets you sell, or the church property you clean is more than it seems to be at first glance. Human communities are not built on grand theories about the "brotherhood of man", but by women who bake bread together and men who ref basketball leagues together day-in and day-out, decade after decade, seeking no more reward than the good of the local church. Moreover, since all of life is sacred, these so-called "social activities" need no justification. They are as spiritual as any Bible study ever was. However, they do teach a lesson: We come to God together or not at all. And Christian community involves the whole person, not just some "spiritual" part.

We in the West have lost our theology of worship at the same time as we have become mobile and "multicultural." There appears to be a connec-

LETTER II

tion between rootless mobility and rootless faith. (Is it a coincidence that rootless America, a nation of immigrants, has provided the fertile soil for more cults and sects to grow in than any other place on earth or in history?) In contrast, there seems to be a connection between the changeless village life of ethnic Orthodox communities and the changeless life of the Spirit.

We worship Persons, not ideas, and those Persons (the Trinity) use people, not things, to bring about the Kingdom of God on earth. It seems that for people to be fully human they must be in true familial communion with not only God but each other. "It is not good that the man should be alone.... And they [were] ... breaking bread with one accord ... [in] singleness of heart" (Genesis 2:18; Acts 2:46).

As ever,
Frank

LETTER III

Dear Fr. Aristotle,

I spoke to a woman the other day who is a recent convert to Orthodoxy from the Episcopalian Protestant denomination. By the grace of God, her whole parish has converted to Orthodoxy. They have kept their priest, who now has been ordained as an Orthodox priest. This woman made an interesting comment to me. She said, "It's wonderful; now that our parish has become Orthodox, we don't really have to change anything! We get to keep everything the way it was, only now we don't have to be part of a church that allows the ordination of women and homosexuals." I asked the woman what it meant to her to be Orthodox, since, according to her, she and her parish did not have to change anything. She did not have an answer. Perhaps she did not understand my question.

It seems to me that some converts seem to think that they have joined "another denomination." Or perhaps they believe that Orthodoxy is just a more conservative version of their old Protestant or Roman faith. This is quite an astonishing idea, though I understand it all too well. I have had, and no doubt still have, many misconceptions about the Orthodox Church. We all learn slowly.

One of the things I have slowly begun to learn is that the Orthodox Church is not just another version of Western Christianity. Orthodoxy is not merely Roman Catholicism or Protestantism *Plus*! Rather, Orthodoxy is a *profoundly different* religion. For one thing, because of the Orthodox understanding of the unity of body and soul, we Orthodox view the Incarnation in quite a different way than Western Christians do, whether they are Roman Catholic or Protestant.

Our Orthodox understanding of the unity of the spiritual and physical world rests on our belief that Christ was—and is—*fully* God and *fully* man. Nothing was given up by either of Christ's two natures to accommodate the other. We believe in the *unity* of reality. Above all, we believe in the *unity* of the Trinity. We hold that God is beyond, yet within, His creation. While we do not confuse the Creator with His creation, we believe that His

LETTER III

presence permeates all of Creation. Therefore, we understand the physical world, even in its "fallen" state, to be sacred and as being redeemed. As a consequence, we put a far greater emphasis on the goodness of the created world than Western Christians do. This emphasis manifests itself in many ways but is most obvious in our Orthodox expression of liturgical and physical sacramental worship. We Orthodox Christians believe that the Fathers, such as St. Maximos the Confessor, were speaking the Truth when they taught that the soul and body are truly one.

> *"Just as soul and body combine to produce a human being, so practice of the virtues and contemplation together constitute a unique spiritual wisdom."*
> (St. Maximos the Confessor, "Fourth Century on Various Texts, 90," The Philokalia, *vol. II, p. 257, translated by G.E.H. Palmer, Philip Sherrard, Kallistos Ware, London, 1990)*

The Western, Augustinian idea is very different than that of St. Maximos and the Eastern Fathers. It is that the body is a mere worthless husk inhabited by the fallen immortal soul, which is completely separate from its mortal "shell."

This and much, much more makes a *huge* difference to the way we view even the small details in the Liturgy and the rubrics of worship. These details reflect a whole way of seeing reality.

To the Orthodox the physical world *matters*. It matters because we sense the presence of the Divine in all of creation. It is impossible that sacramental truth, evolved from a fundamentally mistaken Latin-Western theology that has belittled the truth and beauty of the created world in favor of a Manichean "spirituality" can remain the same or unchanged within Orthodoxy. If it does so, it is not Orthodox. That is not to say that we do not all grow slowly into understanding and enlightenment. We do. But in order to grow, one must at least acknowledge the need to learn more, to become more.

LETTER III

Before the Schism the Western Church was Orthodox. There is no evidence that the Western Orthodox Fathers—for instance, St. Irenaios of Lyon—differed with the Eastern Fathers' view of reality. There is no question of Western versus Eastern Orthodoxy. Indeed, it is ironic that some of the most highly regarded saints of the Western, Latin Church, like Francis of Assisi, were more Orthodox in spirit than they were Western. This is true of some modern Protestant "saints" as well. The late writer C. S. Lewis was certainly more Orthodox in many of his views and attitudes than he was Protestant. (If you doubt this, read his book, *The Great Divorce*.)

Converts like myself from a Western background, particularly a highly developed liturgical Western background that has a passing resemblance to Orthodoxy, have a lot to change, learn, and adjust to in Orthodoxy. I know. I grew up Presbyterian but attended the Anglican Church in England and its sister, the Episcopal Church, in America for more than ten years. I am still groping my way moment-by-moment from that experience into the Orthodox way.

I have found that the "small" differences between the East and West turn out to be not small at all. The mystical, nondogmatic, nontheological, apophatic, nonphilosophical Eastern approach to the Truth is one of *being*, *doing*, and *becoming*, not one of reason or dogmatic theology. Orthodoxy addresses the whole person as no Western church does. And the Orthodox way is the way of the community of all believers, not an individualistic or subjective quest for salvation. Moreover, Orthodoxy involves parts of the person that the Western churches hardly acknowledge.

We Orthodox believe that we become Christians by imitation of Christ, the Theotokos, the Apostles, and the Saints, not through intellectual assent to dogmatic propositions. We believe that we learn Truth through Divine revelation to our *spiritual* intellect, not through bare reason. In other words, we do not believe in a theologically *filtered* faith. We believe in direct, *unfiltered* access to the Truth through grace, as it is revealed to us within the discipline of ascetic and sacramental struggle.

LETTER III

As St. Maximos the Confessor writes:

"Who enlightened you with faith in the holy, coessential and adorable Trinity? Or who made known to you the incarnate dispensation of one of the Holy Trinity? Who taught you about the inner essences of incorporeal beings, or about the origin and consummation of the visible world, or about the resurrection from the dead and eternal life, or about the glory of the kingdom of heaven and the dreadful judgment? Was it not the grace of Christ dwelling in you, which is the pledge of the Holy Spirit? What is greater than this grace? What is more noble than this wisdom and knowledge? What is more lofty than these promises? But if we are lazy and negligent, and if we do not cleanse ourselves from the passions which defile us, blinding our intellect and so preventing us from seeing the inner nature of these realities more clearly than the sun, let us blame ourselves and not deny the indwelling of grace."
("Fourth Century on Love, 77," The Philokalia, vol. II, p. 110)

The Orthodox way produces both outward and inward differences between the West and East in worship, liturgy, and in the whole approach to authority within the Church. For instance, we believe the Holy Spirit leads our bishops and us *directly* through grace. We do not believe we are led by a "Vicar of Christ," a pope (or an ecumenical patriarch) who speaks for Christ *ex-cathedra*.

The Orthodox belief in direct access to Truth within the communal discipline of sacramental life changes the way we understand the world around us. It changes the way we view the arts, worship, work, and human relationships. And it changes our understanding of the sacraments drastically. We do not view them as merely symbolic or as magical acts. We understand them to be a direct means of mystical enlightenment through grace.

It seems to me that converts like myself and would-be converts should

18

LETTER III

be encouraged to explore honestly the many significant differences between the Latin West and Orthodox East. I sometimes think that a misguided Protestant spirit of evangelical triumphalism, which perhaps puts too much stock in numbers and growth, *a la* "born-again experience," and a Roman Catholic-style ecumenist triumphalism which wants to bring "union between all Christians" leads some Orthodox to make almost disingenuous attempts to minimize the differences between the East and West.

It seems to me that a growth-at-any-price and unity-at-any-price mentality is a dangerous trend for the Orthodox. In my opinion, the Orthodox life is a struggle for spiritual quality, not quantity. Better one holy monk than one thousand enthusiastic converts to a false, Westernized "Orthodoxy." And better one pure Orthodox community than a thousand bureaucrats signing documents that purport to "unite all Christians."

This is *not* to say that we have no need for more aggressive Orthodox evangelism. We do. But our Orthodox evangelistic efforts must be Orthodox, not just warmed-over imitations of Roman or Protestant methods.

The Orthodox Church is not a democracy, nor is it a product that needs to be promoted. Truth is *Truth*, and numerical growth for its own sake is the opposite of the ascetic struggle that marks spiritual conversion. According to the Fathers, to be saved takes a lifetime of struggle that only *begins* at baptism and chrismation. Getting people into the Church is the easiest part of all. Helping sinful, foolish, misinformed converts like myself become fully Orthodox is the hard part.

I remember a discussion I had with Bishop Methodios of Boston. At the time we were talking about His Grace's advice to Protestant pastors who want to convert to the Orthodox Church. I remember His Grace saying that he thought that before a Protestant pastor could become an Orthodox priest, he should go spend "at least a year on Mt. Athos at a monastery so that he can get a real understanding of what Orthodoxy is."

LETTER III

At the time I thought that His Grace was joking. It has taken me a number of years to fully realize my bishop's wisdom. After an all-too-short pilgrimage to several monastic centers in the Holy Land and on Mt. Athos, I now know what Bishop Methodios was talking about. My experience was life changing. Truly we converts from Protestantism and Roman Catholicism have little idea of the depth and beauty of Orthodoxy. Truly there is far more to the Orthodox Church than at first meets the eye. And, truly, an Orthodox priest must become far more than simply a "good pastor." Bishop Methodios was right. The heart of the Orthodox way of being is not found in seminaries or ecumenical dialogues but in the monastic life of the Church.

From the Protestant point of view of church-growth-at-any-price, a suggestion that a potential convert, especially a pastor with a whole ready-made flock, should be encouraged to go to a monastery for a year seems impractical. But Orthodoxy *is* impractical! It is too deep, too real, too ancient to be neatly packaged into an instant "method". Moreover, its theology exists in the liturgical life of the Church, not in textbooks.

Orthodoxy cannot be studied—only lived. It is in the depths of Orthodox mystery, not in a set of new theological rules, that the Pearl of Great Price is hidden.

I suppose that from a Protestant or post-Vatican II Roman Catholic point of view, the woman I spoke to who saw no need to change anything after her conversion was right. If only the juridical salvation of the soul matters; if we individually worship "in our hearts"; if the externals—the community of faith, the flesh, and the world—do not matter or have been rendered meaningless or worse by "original sin"; if conversion is emphasized at the expense of ascetic struggle; and if theology can be learned from a book; then, of course, how one worships does not matter, as long as one is sincere.

But if the Trinity is One, and if both the Son and the Holy Spirit proceed from the Father; if Christ is the Lover of Mankind, and if He came in

LETTER III

the flesh; then the world, the externals, the flesh matter. And if this is so, the sacraments matter, not because they are magical—quite the reverse is true—but because *all* of creation is sacred. And if these things are true, then what the Orthodox Church *is* matters as much as what it teaches. What we *do* matters as much as what we think. What we *feel* matters least of all. We who convert late in life have a lot to learn and a lot to change.

As ever,
Frank

LETTER IV

Dear Fr. Aristotle,

It appears that there is a certain confusion inside, as well as outside, the Orthodox Church about our unique identity. This confusion exists, at least in part, because we Orthodox believe in what appears to be a contradiction. We believe in the mysterious grace of God, and, at the same time, we believe that God's mercy extends beyond the Orthodox Church to all people. This latter point is illustrated by the way that Christ's mercy touched the thief on the cross who had not prayed a "sinner's prayer" of repentance or been baptized. Yet the thief was promised paradise. (The monks say that the last thing he stole was salvation!)

Yet in spite of God's mercy beyond the visible limits of the Church, we believe that within the Orthodox Church the means of salvation are uniquely available. So while we would never judge an individual's salvation on the basis of his "keeping all the rules," or "being in our church," we do indeed clearly declare what is and is not the Church and what is or is not the Truth.

We believe that only in the context of the Orthodox Church is the fullness of God's grace to be found, notwithstanding that His mercy to all mankind knows no boundaries. It is this paradox of our believing in God's boundless mercy and at the same time in the fullness of His indivisible, pure Orthodox Church that I believe confounds the Western rationalistic and scholastic mind.

From the Western point of view, we Orthodox are perceived as "weak" because we say the mercy of God extends to all mankind regardless of theology or dogma. Yet Western Christians find the Orthodox "harsh" in that we forbid non-Orthodox from receiving the sacraments of the Church.

As we Orthodox defend the purity of the Orthodox faith, the West is scandalized. Yet when we speak of the mystery of salvation, the juridical West, in love with its scientific "certainties," philosophies, dogmatic laws, and theologies, is confounded. However, understood within the Orthodox

LETTER IV

context, this paradox is not a self-contradiction. It is explained by the character of God, Who is beyond reason and beyond human understanding.

As St. Maximos the Confessor writes:

> *"God is one, unoriginate, incomprehensible, possessing completely the total potentiality of being, altogether excluding notions of when and how, inaccessible to all, and not to be known through natural image by any creature."*
> *("First Century on Theology, 1," The Philokalia, vol. II, p. 114)*

To some people, some of the time Orthodoxy seems the most "open" and the most "ecumenical" of religions. To other people, at other times it seems the most "narrow." I would say that both perceptions of Orthodoxy are true. In matters of faith and individual salvation, we Orthodox are the least dogmatic because we acknowledge the incomprehensibility of God. As a result, we never put dogma or theology ahead of or above God, as if we could explain God to God and tell Him whom to save! Yet on the other hand, we believe that only the Orthodox Church is the Christ—bearing community on earth in its fullness. Only in Her are found the sacraments, and only in Her is found the sure road to salvation. We believe this is so, even though we joyfully affirm that God's mercy extends beyond the Orthodox Church and that God, Who is not to be known through any natural image, is not confined by His Church, though He dwells in Her. Yet we also affirm that God's mercy is not limited to only those people in the Church. At the same time we believe that salvation comes only though the Orthodox Church in both history and sacrament.

Salvation comes only through the Orthodox Church historically, because only the Orthodox Church has preserved the Scriptures and the right teaching of the Apostles in their fullness. And salvation comes only through the Orthodox Church in the sacraments, because only the Orthodox Church has preserved the proper apostolic use of them.

LETTER IV

Those who do not understand how very consistent the Orthodox Church is in spite of the Orthodox embrace of paradox fail to see that even if we Orthodox have no juridical, dogmatic theology, as the West understands these things, nevertheless we have a very complete theology in our own way. This theology is our liturgical tradition. It is non-negotiable, even though it is "poetic" rather than "Germanic," so to speak.

The reason that the West fails to understand that a poetic, liturgical tradition is as real and binding as written dogma is because the average Western person does not take poetry as seriously as he takes math, science, and law. To the Western person, reality must be "scientifically" described, explained, and quantified to be understood, to be "official." This is why the West thinks of us as "weak," theologically. They equate mystery with indecisiveness and poetry with imprecision. But Orthodox apophatic silence and appreciation of the mystery of God and acknowledgment of paradox is the "weakness" of the still, small voice of the God Who is inaccessible to all.

We Orthodox regard the scientific West as blind. We regard the West as blind not only to religion but blind to the actual truth of the way things really are. In fact, from the Orthodox point of view, it is the mechanistic, mathematical, "scientific" view that is a personally held, subjective, irrational faith. To us love, poetry, mystery, and iconic beauty more accurately describe the fullness of reality than math and science do.

It is our very different way of understanding reality and of seeing and being that we Orthodox must learn and relearn and impart to others. Moreover, we Orthodox who live in the Western, materialistic desert of non-being need to understand the unique ability of the Orthodox Tradition to teach us to discern the inner, hidden beauty and meaning in the world around us.

As ever,
Frank

LETTER V

Dear Fr. Aristotle,

It seems to me that we in the West have lost our ability to see with our spiritual intellects because we trust in our reason and our emotions. Moreover, the West's uncritical acceptance of the materialistic and scientific view of reality that was popularized, if not invented, by the seventeenth-century Western philosophers and scientists like René Descartes and Francis Bacon, has proved disastrous and thoroughly unchristian.

As a result of blindly accepting the "scientific approach" to reality, we have lost our desire and ability for ascetic struggle. We want our Christianity made rational, understandable, emotionally pleasing, and easy. We want "Christianity Lite." This is why the Western churches have reduced spirituality to a study in psychological well-being. This is why we have reduced faith to feelings or easy dogmatic rules. And this is why the post-Vatican II Roman Catholic Church has destroyed itself in the process of debunking its own mystical traditions of monastic struggle, fasting, prayer, and contemplation in favor of so-called "people's Masses" and "user-friendly," easy-to-understand, rational pop-Christianity.

It is easier and more fun to learn to strum a guitar badly than to practice a Gregorian chant. It is easier to dress in street clothes than die to the world in an authentic monastery or convent. This is perhaps why some converts used to an undemanding Christianity think that we can be in the Orthodox Church but not of it. Perhaps some converts think that we do not need to change more than our parish's stationary or where we go for Bible study!

We have gotten so used to a simplistic and formulaic religion that when we encounter authentic complexity, history, and paradox, we do not know what to make of it. The idea that our salvation is going to be achieved over a lifetime takes some getting used to for those of us accustomed to easy-to-remember "pat" answers for every question.

For those of us who thought we could be saved by the magic of keeping

LETTER V

a few Roman Catholic rules or by the magic of the "born-again experience," it is a rude shock to wake up and find that in order to be saved we will have to become Christ, and that this epic transformation is going to take most of us all of this life *and* the next. A confrontation with the mystery of reality is a frightening thing.

As ever,
Frank

LETTER VI

Dear Fr. Aristotle,

Thank you for your letter asking for my opinion on what to do about the fact that your parish council president has proposed the use of your parish hall and Hellenic cultural center as the venue for hosting a fund-raising banquet for the Democratic Party. You mention that a well-known Democrat of Greek origin is to be the featured fund-raising speaker. I understand that since your parish council president is also your community's largest contributor, that this, indeed as you put it in your letter, is an "extremely delicate matter." I sympathize with your dilemma! However, I believe that you are right when you say that this political event is inappropriate.

For any church to use its premises—or to allow them to be rented—for a brazenly political event involving any party is, I believe, a misbegotten idea. I also believe it is reasonable of you to object to the politics of the invited speaker who is, as you write me, "well known as a supporter of legalized abortion on demand, government funding of abortion, fetal experimentation, homosexual rights, and the usual social agenda of most secular, liberal Democratic politicians these days."

You should point out to your parish council president that even if you agreed with the pro-abortion political views of the invited speaker (which, of course, no Orthodox Christian ever could), you feel that it is a serious error in judgment for your Greek Orthodox church (or any Orthodox, for that matter) to allow the Church's good name to be linked to a specific political party, much less to raise money for it on church premises. (This, of course, is different than the need to encourage practical involvement with programs that may coincidentally have a political dimension, like feeding the poor or providing a Christian alternative to abortion. In such cases the intent is to be an icon of the love of Christ, not to help a political party. Such activities are in agreement with the teaching of the Church Fathers.)

Your letter raises two serious questions. The first is the question of

LETTER VI

whether mere national background makes a person Orthodox. After all, except for his Greek ancestry, what other reason would your parish council president have for inviting this speaker to your community since his views, and those of his party, can scarcely be described as Christian, let alone Orthodox? The second question is whether or not it is appropriate for an Orthodox church to ever host a political event, even for candidates who are truly Orthodox in spirit as well as name.

Fr. Aristotle, ask your parish council president if he believes that having your community become embroiled with the day-to-day politics of secular American society is in the true interest of your parish. Ask him if it is appropriate for an Orthodox community to endorse a candidate because of his or her ethnic background, regardless of the moral beliefs of the candidate or the moral content of that candidate's political party platform. (If he thinks it is appropriate, then ask him where he would draw the line on working with politicians whose moral views are out of step with Orthodox Tradition. If he says that he would never draw such a line, then ask him what it means to him to be Orthodox. If he says he would draw the line over some issues, then ask him what could be a bigger moral issue than the sanctity of human life.) Moreover, ask him if he feels it is right to alienate his fellow Orthodox who may not share this candidate's political beliefs.

I know that this presents you with a big problem because your council president is heavily involved with your church as well as with the Democratic Party. (According to your letter, his family has just paid for the narthex renovation as well!) Nevertheless, it seems to me the height of short-sighted folly for your Orthodox community to squander its unique patristic inheritance by allowing your church buildings to be used for overtly partisan, political purposes.

Surely the Church should be above squalid cozying-up to worldly power? Surely the best interests of the Church are not foremost in the hearts of Orthodox Democratic, Republican, or other politicians who would stoop so low as to use their Church for political gain?

LETTER VI

It seems that no Orthodox political candidate or political fund-raiser who truly has the good of the Church at heart would want to see Her tangled up with political pandering. The Church has enough of Her own baggage without the enemies and problems of secular politicians. The old adage, those who lie down with dogs get up with fleas, seems appropriate.

Please do not misunderstand me. I believe it is our duty, as citizens, to be involved politically and to vote our moral conscience. And I believe that it is a good thing to run for political office. In fact, I wish more Christians were actively involved in every level of government. But what we are discussing in this context is not the political involvement of individual Orthodox in our nation's affairs, but the Church Herself becoming a political creature.

It disturbs me that your parish council president, who you say in your letter is a "well-educated lawyer of distinguished Greek ancestry" has apparently learned nothing from his own recent Greek history. Perhaps it would be well to remind him that Mahomet II, the Turkish Sultan, did the Orthodox no favor by deliberately politicizing the Orthodox office of Patriarch! (According to Islamic tradition, a "nation" is determined by its religion. Consequently, Mahomet II, in his role of Sultan, regarded the Greek Orthodox Patriarch as both spiritual *and* political head of the Greek people.) Subsequent historic events proved that this deliberate confusion of the political with the spiritual has had disastrous consequences for the Orthodox.

One of these disastrous consequences is that sometimes the more worldly and ambitious of the Patriarchs of Constantinople have played along with the un-Orthodox confusion of worldly and ecclesiastical power and have ascribed to themselves powers that the Church gives no bishop. As such, some Patriarchs of Constantinople pretended that they "speak for the Church"—as if they were a kind of Orthodox pope. This has caused nothing but trouble and has so confused some Orthodox that they truly believe that the Bishop of Constantinople is the "head of the Orthodox Church." Of course this is *not* the Orthodox tradition. Each Orthodox

LETTER VI

bishop has equal authority with every other bishop, though some ancient sees of the Church have greater moral authority when it comes to speaking to issues of doctrine. However, this moral authority is not supposed to have a political dimension. That it sometimes does is a Turkish corruption, something to be corrected, not promoted.

Remind your parish president that it was the Sultan, not the Patriarch, who transformed the Orthodox Church into an administrative system run out of Constantinople through which the Sultan could control, consolidate, and organize his ill-gotten empire. Remind him that the Patriarchs were finally reduced to purchasing their office from the Sultans. Politicians, it seems, have always found the Orthodox Church "useful!"

As the study of history shows, when the Orthodox Church helps the State, even when that State or its representatives are Greek or Russian, it often has proved to be a one-way bargain in favor of the State. The great historian, Sir Steven Runciman describes just such a one-way bargain involved in the politicizing and corruption of the Orthodox Church under the Turks. This corruption was often aided and abetted by the Orthodox themselves, who were all too eager to profit from dubious and lucrative political connections. In fact, to Runciman, the Phanariots—in other words, the politically powerful and well-connected Greeks who were best placed to both influence and profit from the Turks *and* the Greek Church—were ultimately to blame for the eventual infiltration of the Orthodox Church by Western influences in the eighteenth and nineteenth centuries. (The word *Phanariot* is derived from the name *Phanar*, which is the area in which the Orthodox Patriarchate of Constantinople is located.)

Runciman's account of Panariot misdeeds is reminiscent of our own day. It seems to me that we, too, have some ambitious and politically well-connected Orthodox laymen, priests, bishops, and hierarchs in our midst who seem to be much better suited to Vatican-style politics, business, and Western philosophy than to the Orthodox way of living.

LETTER VI

Sir Steven Runciman writes:

"The strength of the Byzantine Church had been the presence of a highly educated laity that was deeply interested in religion. Now [in the 17th and 18th centuries] the laity began to despise the traditions of the Church. . . . Under Phanariot influence many of the higher ecclesiastics followed the modernist trend. In the old days Orthodoxy had preferred to concentrate on eternal things and modestly to refuse to clothe faith in the trappings of modish philosophy. The Phanariots, in their desire to impress the West, had no use for such old-fashioned notions. . . . The Phanariots with their political and intellectual ambitions threatened to damage what had hitherto been the greatest asset of the Orthodox Church. If there was no Reformation in Eastern Christendom, nor even any heretical movement as powerful as that of the Cathars in the medieval West, it was because the Church had never lost touch with the people. . . . But the Turkish conquest had obliged the Patriarchate to take on secular duties. Its high officials had to be administrators. Worldly laymen were more useful than spiritually minded ecclesiastics. From the seventeenth century onwards, under the influence of the Phanariots, this laicization was increased. The rich merchants of Constantinople, on whose benefactions the Patriarch depended for his financial security, coveted posts at his Court for their relatives and began to use the offices for their political ends. . . . Their [Westernized] education made them unsympathetic with the older traditions of the Church. By the eighteenth century it was a matter of pride for them to be versed in Western philosophy and the rationalism fashionable at the time."
(The Great Church in Captivity, *Cambridge, 1968, pp. 377-87)*

It is understandable that Greek Orthodox Christians in the Ottoman empire, under threat of death, might—however reluctantly—allow themselves to be used politically by the Sultans. (I suppose the same could be

LETTER VI

said of the Russian "KGB bishops.") That Orthodox in a relatively *free* country would choose to be politically manipulated is quite another matter.

The new Greek-American "Phanariots" may gain some short-term advantage for the Orthodox, or at least the Greek, community by playing politics with the Orthodox Church, but it seems that in the long run the Church will be the loser. In fact, in several notable instances the political association of certain ethnic Greek-American politicians with Orthodox clergy and the endorsement of certain candidates by clergy has caused scandal and lasting harm to the credibility of the Orthodox in America, both inside and outside the Orthodox community.

Ultimately the Church's transcendent vision must clash with the mundane and worldly vision of the secular State. More importantly, there is an act of spiritual desecration at work when the Church is used for anything but its own unique, apostolic, sacramental mission.

As St. Neilos the Ascetic writes:

> *"We gain nothing, therefore, by our decision to renounce earthly things if we do not abide by it, but continue to be attracted by such things."*
> *("Ascetic Discourse,"* The Philokalia, *vol. I, p. 236)*

If I were you, Fr. Aristotle, I would refuse to allow your council president to have his way in this matter. If your stand results in the loss of his financial support—so be it. In fact, it might be a good object lesson to your congregation to see that it is more important to live the Orthodox life than to be "successful" in worldly terms. (Again, let me emphasize that I am not saying anything against Orthodox who choose to run for office. I think this can be an excellent calling. Nor am I saying that we Orthodox should not speak out boldly on the issues of the day. I believe we should. I am just speaking about Orthodox trying to embroil their church politically.) Your parish should see that their priest puts the spiritual inheritance of the Church ahead of all other interests.

As ever,
Frank

LETTER VI

P.S. I highly recommend that you read *The Great Church in Captivity*, the book by Sir Steven Runciman that I quoted above. It is a wonderful and very sympathetic history of the Orthodox Church and also, as the quote illustrates, has a direct application to our present-day situation in North America. In many ways we, too, are in "captivity" in an alien land and risk being corrupted by Western, intellectual folly and Westernized "Orthodox" who see their church as a useful political tool.

LETTER VII

Dear Fr. Aristotle,

Thank you for your last letter. I am delighted to hear that the political fund-raising event has been canceled! I applaud your courage. I am, however, sorry to learn that your parish council president resigned over the matter and that several leading families have left your community. I am particularly saddened by the fact that you write that your bishop sided with your council president. (I hope this is not because your president is a large contributor to "Leadership 100" and the Greek diocese!) I pray that your bishop's threat to send you to a "small parish in Lapland" is not carried out! Please keep me posted. Now, as to your question about my views on what the "expectation of the Orthodox Church should be in our secular culture," here are a few very incomplete thoughts.

It seems to me that the fundamental error of modern, Western, American society is that it tends to look for political, economic, psychological, or social solutions to what are, in fact, spiritual problems. To put it bluntly, tax rates, social welfare programs, building prisons, dispensing condoms, paying for abortions, installing metal detectors in schools, and repeating mantras about cultural diversity, racial harmony, sexual preference, the brotherhood of man, and community will not change the heart of one individual. Thus, these actions will not change our society's slide toward social, family, sexual, and civil breakdown. In short, coercive methods of social engineering, like encouraging abortions or building prisons, are an admission of the failure of our spiritual will.

Our society is becoming increasingly coercive because its social programs have failed. They have failed because they have tried to provide secular solutions to fundamentally spiritual problems. It seems to me that coercion is the last "answer" to social chaos for those who have no moral base on which to build self-government.

The secularistic confusion between spiritual problems and social problems has even infected some religious people. A recent example of this is the way in which the Roman Catholic bishops of North America seem to have confused the welfare agenda of the left wing of the Democratic Party

LETTER VII

with the Kingdom of God. Similarly, conservative right-wing Protestants have apparently confused the "American dream" with the biblical call to be a "city set on a hill" and a "light unto the nations." The platform of the Republican Party, not to mention the Constitution, is treated by many right-wing Protestants as revealed truth. To the Right, the American founding fathers have become analogous to the Fathers of the Church.

Unfortunately, it seems that we Orthodox at times also have succumbed to the worldly temptation to confuse political and spiritual problems. It appears that most of our continuing participation in the so-called ecumenical movement is now far more relevant to politics than spirituality. And it seems that our Orthodox involvement in such failed and compromised bodies as the World and National Council of Churches may possibly have more to do with our desire to be respectable in the West than with a desire to bear uncompromising witness to the Truth.

Perhaps we should search our hearts on these matters. An excellent book on just how politicized the World and National Council of Churches have become is *From Mainline to Sideline* by K. L. Billingsley (Ethics and Public Policy Center, University Press of America, 1990). It is well worth reading. We Orthodox should at least know who we are in bed with.

The task or expectation of the Orthodox Church in society is *not*, in my opinion, to try and reconcile Christianity to the materialistic view of things or to reconcile Orthodoxy to Western Christianity, even if this is done under the slogan of Orthodox witness. It seems to me that the only authentic Orthodox witness is a call to Roman Catholics, Protestants, and other Western Christians to return to the Orthodox way. This call is *evangelistic*, not *ecumenist*. The Orthodox Church must accept converts but not bend to meet them, or the world, halfway. Rather than looking endlessly for middle ground, we must offer the non-Orthodox what we Orthodox alone can provide: the restoration of the sense of the sacred to a severely desecrated and desacralized culture. In order to accomplish this task, we must begin by teaching the desacralized Western world that all of creation is sacred.

LETTER VII

St. Maximos the Confessor writes:

> *"The Holy Spirit is present unconditionally in all things, in that He embraces all things, provides for all, and vivifies the natural seeds within them."*
> *("First Century of Various Texts,"* The Philokalia, *vol. II, p. 180)*

St. Maximos expresses the Orthodox understanding of how God imbues creation with meaning and how He actively sustains all created things. I believe that the restoration of this understanding is a vocation the Orthodox Church *alone* can fill, and this should be the true expectation of the Orthodox in our secular society.

There is no halfway meeting point between the Western scientific-political-materialistic worldview and Orthodoxy. Either one looks at reality with the eyes of Orthodox faith, or one does not. Worship, community, education, marriage, family life, friendship—these things that form the expression of the essence of human life can only be understood in only one of two ways:

(1) as a manifestation of material and psychological determinism

or

(2) as a manifestation, or archetype, of Truth.

These opposing ways of seeing reality (what we might think of as St. Maximos the Confessor versus Augustine, Calvin, Freud, Darwin, and Nietzsche) radically change the way we perceive life and how we act. For instance, we can look at education in only one of two ways:

(1) as a preparation to become a "productive worker"

or

LETTER VII

(2) as the realization, over a lifetime, of the fulfillment of the beautiful and sacred intellectual-spiritual gift God has given each of us.

The secular man deludes himself into believing that problems produced by modern society, such as those in secular education, have technical solutions (i.e. word processors on every desk, the "information highway," and new philosophies or methods of education).

Similarly, the secularized Orthodox are also deluded when they abandon the purity of Truth in favor of pursuing political-theological solutions, such as ecumenism, to what are fundamentally spiritual problems caused by false belief. The problem is not one of mending an historic "misunderstanding" but of two radically opposite ways of perceiving reality. Only a secularist who no longer believes in Truth could think that such differences as the ones that divide Western Latin Christianity and the Eastern Orthodox could be negotiated. This supposedly religious idea is secular relativism, pure and simple.

In its search for technical solutions to what are fundamentally spiritual problems, the secular world and some of the secularized Orthodox have reduced all of life to a series of "useful," or utilitarian, techniques. These techniques are used to try and change human nature and society and to bring about peace on earth. Secular man sees no need for a change of heart—only a need for a change of method. But the Orthodox view is very different. It seems to me that Truth is our quest and beauty is our desire. Our "technique" is ascetic struggle and prayer, not politics, ecumenism, or negotiation. We are not primarily interested in the utility of things—much less in utopian pipe dreams—but in their essence, in the Truth they represent.

As St. Maximos writes:

> *"From created beings we come to know their Cause. . . . The Holy Spirit is not absent from any created being."*
> *("First Century of Various Texts,"* The Philokalia, *vol. II, p. 180)*

LETTER VII

Creation is filled with the Holy Spirit—*that* is why it is meaningful and sacred. We understand life as an archetype of the eternal order of things established by the Creator. We do not see our lives as merely a "means to an end." We believe that all we do has meaning *in itself* because the Spirit is present in us. We Orthodox should not be interested in saving societies but in saving the Spirit-filled individuals who dwell in the world with us, because "the Holy Spirit is not absent from any created being." We Orthodox should not be so naive as to believe that the loss of the sense of the sacred meaning of life, in evidence all around us in our social pathologies, can be made up for by technical tricks, redistribution of wealth, or an overhaul of the health care system. We know that nothing can be resolved or changed without first addressing the basic question of meaning. To us, life is not meaningful because of what we can produce or accomplish, but because we value the sacred worthiness of the act of life itself.

We believe in the intrinsic worth, beauty, and goodness of the created world. And we believe this life has meaning and beauty because it is part of a high order of reality. We believe that salvation is a journey through this life toward the life to come and that all of existence forms one unbroken chain, from the least subatomic particle to the very throne of God. We believe that all of life, all of creation, all experiences, are sacred, or none of them are.

St. Athanasius describes the journey of salvation in very physical terms as the restoration of a damaged portrait. It is this quest, this lifelong act of incremental restoration involving our whole person and the whole of creation, that engages our attention as Orthodox.

St. Athanasius writes:

> *"You know what happens when a portrait that has been painted on a panel becomes obliterated through external stains. The artist does not throw away the panel, but the subject of the portrait has to come and sit for it again, and then the likeness is redrawn on the*

same material. Even so was it with the All-holy Son of God. He, the Image of the Father, came and dwelt in our midst, in order that He might renew mankind made after Himself. . . . The Savior of us all, the Word of God, in His great love took to Himself a body and moved as Man among men, meeting their senses, so to speak, half way. He became Himself an object for the senses, so that those who were seeking God in sensible things might apprehend the Father through the works which He, the Word of God, did in the body."
(On the Incarnation, Crestwood, New York, 1953, pp. 41-43)

The secular culture that surrounds us tends to place little or no value on the living of life as a worthwhile act of restoration. This is because secular man no longer believes that the Spirit dwells in him and in creation. To the secular person, life is wholly utilitarian, wholly result-oriented. He cares little or knows nothing of the true sacramental purpose of life. But for us Orthodox, the act and the result are one and the same. It is by *being* something that we *become* that thing. It is by *doing* God's will—in other words, in keeping His commandments—that we *become* recreated, "repainted," restored to His Image. Therefore, to use education again as an example, we believe that the act of self-discipline, esthetic enjoyment and appreciation, and the learning of wisdom inherent in reading with a hunger and thirst for beauty and Truth is an end in itself. Hence an Orthodox educator would not say, "You'd better learn to read or you'll never get a job!" but rather, "You should learn to read because reading is wonderful! Human creativity is a great and good gift from God."

It seems to me that Christ tells us that the ascetic act of hungering and thirsting after righteousness is *in itself* part of the way of salvation. This, it appears, is what Christ told the rich young ruler in the Gospel story. It was the act of giving all he had to the poor, not the so-called "good" this sacrifice would do, that would be salvific to the rich young ruler. It was his sacred act of charity and ascetic sacrifice, the curbing of his passion of selfishness, that would have initiated him into the Mystery of Faith.

LETTER VII

As St. Maximos the Confessor writes:

> *"He who has put an end to the root of corruption in himself by practicing the virtues is initiated into other more divine experiences."*
> *("First Century On Theology,"* The Philokalia, *vol. II, p. 121)*

According to the Fathers, the spiritual journey is not something only for the Saints. In this regard Saints like St. Seraphim of Sarov are not different from us. (Do you remember how St. Seraphim of Sarov spent one thousand days and nights on a great boulder in the forest near his hermitage in prayer, crying, "Lord, have mercy," and through this struggle was granted a vision of the blessed Theotokos?) For all Orthodox, life should become one thousand days and nights upon a rock, praying, "Lord, have mercy."

If we come to understand each act of life as part of the ascetic struggle, rather than as a utilitarian means to an end, then each act, whether it be prayer, fasting, marriage, education, celibate monastic struggle, work, or suffering, can become the part of our hungering and thirsting after the fullness of God. A large measure of this hungering and thirsting is expressed by a recognition of the beauty and love of God we see revealed in creation. The ascetic life is not one of sorrow and hardship only, but, according to the Fathers, one spent seeing things as they really are. St. Maximos the Confessor writes:

> *"We do not know God from His essence. We know Him rather from the grandeur of His creation and from His providential care for all His creatures. For through these, as though they were mirrors, we may attain insight into His infinite goodness, wisdom and power."*
> *("First Century on Theology,"* The Philokalia, *vol. II, p. 64)*

The problem is, of course, that we fall woefully short of our objective to see reality as God sees it. Nevertheless, we Orthodox must not give in and

LETTER VII

meet the world halfway. Nor must we delude ourselves into thinking that we can come to some "understanding" with the world (or with apostate and falsified Christianity), or come to some common middle ground through dialogue.

As I said, the world believes that psychological, academic, technical, ecumenical, political, or scientific "explanations" and "solutions" exist for all the problems caused by mankind's imperfections, not to mention mankind's stupid ideas! In essence, they believe that we are perfectible by our own efforts without God and that there is no such thing as sin—only various forms of "maladjustment". If we could only find the "right solution" to each problem, they believe that we could become masters of our evolution until we have created a "New Man" and a paradise on earth. But the Gulag, Auschwitz, and the local abortion clinic bear mute testimony to the gross failure of the human engineering and utopian projects of our secular age to produce this "New Man."

We Orthodox know that we are not masters of our destiny. We believe in *synergia*, that mystical element of grace wherein God condescends to meet us and makes it possible for us to hope that we may stand before Him and not be bound and cast out by the angels. Though we are unable, He is able. Though our free will is inadequate, God strengthens our desire for Him and completes by grace what we can only begin by faith.

The principle of the Stone that is rejected becoming the cornerstone of our salvation is lived out in each of us. Only God can meet us halfway. Only God can help us use the daily acts of life, being a bishop, priest, monk, nun, parent, housewife, student, husband, businessman, farmer, author, whatever, to recreate ourselves through Christ, one step at a time, in His Image. This recreation is not achieved by science or theology (much less by an ecumenical bureaucracy!), but by *imitation* and *mystical initiation* into the Holy Way. It is a state of being, not a state of mind. It is a change of heart, not a change of law. It is the result of self-government, not the result of legislation. The goal is salvation, not a "new world order." Salvation is not a man-made product.

LETTER VII

According to the Fathers, salvation is a gift waiting to be discovered:

> *"It was on account of this that our Lord and God Jesus Christ,*
> *showing His love for us, suffered for the whole of mankind and*
> *gave to all men an equal hope of resurrection."*
> *(St. Maximos the Confessor, "First Century on Love," The*
> Philokalia, *vol. II, p. 60)*

The original, uncreated portrait of God is already within each of us.

St. Maximos the Confessor writes:

> *"God made us so that we might become 'partakers of the divine*
> *nature' (2 Pet. 1:4) and sharers in His eternity, and so that we*
> *might come to be like Him (cf. 1 John 3:2) through deification by*
> *grace."*
> *("First Century of Various Texts," The Philokalia, vol. II, p. 173)*

The difference between Orthodoxy and the world is the fact that we actively use Divine sacramental tools to find and restore the kernel of immortality of which the Fathers speak. We trust our fate to this sacramental path rather than to our own cleverness. We seek not only spiritual tools to restore us to God, but we seek to use the ordinary acts of life as part of our spiritual journey. These, too, can contribute to changing our character into Christ's image and likeness. The salvific acts of life can be as varied as reading out loud to our children or disciplining ourselves to finish a tedious task. We have plenty of examples to follow! Think of St. Seraphim of Sarov disciplining himself to care for the nuns—his "children"—at the Diviev convent, in spite of the jealousy of his abbot. Think of St. Mary of Egypt in her parched desert. Think of St. Elizabeth, Grand Duchess of Russia, continuing to nurse the sick, even when she knew that the Communists were going to kill her. Think of the many other unknown New Martyrs of Russia awaiting the resurrection in forgotten, unmarked graves.

LETTER VII

It seems that it is wrong to so spiritualize the Saints' lives that we forget that their ordinary acts also sanctified them. Who is to say that St. Seraphim's salvation was achieved more in fasting than in feeding his beloved wild bears? Who is to say that St. Seraphim's humility in taking the near-fatal beating he received from three thieves was more salvific than his daily patience with jealous bishops and abbots? Who is to say that St. Seraphim's storing up bits of dry Holy Bread for pilgrims was more important than his thanksgiving for the little stream that ran next to his hermitage, whose banks the Saint lovingly maintained with the rocks he gathered in the forest?

The point is that our struggle against our unruly passions and our struggle to practice virtue can be carried on in the midst of so-called ordinary life. Or to put it another way, we have no excuse for not struggling against our passions just because we are in ordinary, rather than monastic, circumstances.

"In each of us the energy of the Spirit is made manifest according to the measure of his faith. (cf Rom. 12:6) Therefore each of us is the steward of his own grace." (St. Maximos the Confessor, "Third Century of Various Texts," The Philokalia, *vol. II, p. 217)*

When the Czar and Czarina came to honor St. Seraphim at his funeral, it was not only because of St. Seraphim's dramatic achievements, the healings and other miracles he had worked through his prayers (much less because of political or bureaucratic achievements in ecumenical dialogue!), but because he had won the internal battle. He had been a good steward of his own grace.

St. Seraphim took the ordinary things of life and used them to transform his character into the image that the Lord would recognize as His own. He discovered what was there all along; the sacred in the ordinary, the kernel of immortality already present in the mortal flesh that falls into the ground and is resurrected.

LETTER VII

For us Orthodox there are no "big" spiritual acts or "little" secular acts. All of life is equally sacred if we will see it for what it is. There is only the everlasting Now, the "I AM" of God. So for us, the so-called result is always the thing we should think of last. The Being, the Act, the Now, is what truly matters. The question we need to ask is not, "What will come of what I am doing?" but rather we should ask, "Am I doing the right thing? Is it good? Is it virtuous?"

Our nonutilitarian approach to life is what separates we Orthodox from the Western secular world that is always calculating the scientific, economic, psychological, or political results of its actions. In contrast to the Orthodox, the Western world has become like an art dealer who knows the price of all the art works in his gallery but does not appreciate the beauty of any of them. Christ, by contrast, is the artist Himself. He knows and loves each portrait, because He has invested Himself in it.

What is the expectation of the Orthodox Church in society? It should live in the eternal present and refuse to mortgage that present for the utilitarian promise of a humanistic utopia, whether this utopia is the invention of Marx, Darwin, Hitler, Stalin, the United Nations, the Pope, or even the World Council of Churches.

It seems to me that we are to realize the imminent expectation of Christ in us. He has come, is coming, and shall come. Why? Because, "pitying our race, moved with compassion for our limitation, unable to endure that death should have the mastery, . . . He took to Himself a body, a human body even as our own" (St. Athanasius, *On the Incarnation*, p. 34).

As ever,
Frank

LETTER VIII

Dear Fr. Aristotle,

I am very sorry to hear you are discouraged. You write, "Sometimes I question everything." You are not alone. Besides personal doubts, the state of Orthodoxy is sometimes enough to discourage anyone.

Besides being sorry for you, I am sorry to be writing to you *today*! I would much rather be out in my garden! You see, in June everything that has been a promise is fulfilled. It is the season to be out of doors, not at a desk. (This is not irrelevant to your discouragements. Be patient and hear me out!)

In my garden I have planted many trees, vines, and shrubs. I have also let certain areas go very wild indeed. June is a month that I delight in. All the birds and animals who take advantage of my gardening have been very busy having babies, laying eggs, and digging burrows in March, April, and May. Finally, in June, they begin to show me the results of their work. They show me their families.

In my grapevine, a mother and father morningdove took turns, all through the cold days of April and May, sitting on their two white eggs. The mother actually did most of the sitting, but morningdoves, who mate for life and care for each other most attentively, work together to raise their young. The father feeds the mother and will sometimes take a turn on the eggs.

After the eggs hatch and the babies are about one week old, the father trades places with the mother and allows her, at long last, to stretch her cramped wings. Imagine how stiff they are after more than three weeks of sitting absolutely still, absolutely quiet, so as not to draw attention to herself!

The doves are the color of a pair of soft, tan suede shoes. They seem to melt into the dappled shadows of the grape arbor. You do not notice the mother dove unless you look straight at her. She makes no noise at all, though the father sits crooning nearby.

Above all, the mother dove is patient and brave. She will not leave her nest. She will not abandon her young. When I first visited her, she sat rigid, her sides heaving in and out as her heart beat faster and her breaths quickened in fright. But, gradually, like all the many nesting birds in my garden, the mother morningdove got used to me watching her and eventually seemed to take my presence in stride.

This year seems to have been particularly blessed. We not only have the doves nesting in the garden, but many other birds as well. There are a pair of blue jays, two families of mockingbirds, three pairs of sparrows, a family of martins, many, many grackles, various ducks, house finches, warblers, a pair of cardinals, and, most amazing of all, a wonderful pair of woodpeckers in the old pear tree next to the back door.

Besides the birds, we have two warrens of woodchucks, a large family of chipmunks, many squirrels, a tribe of rabbits, a couple of opossums, and a red fox. (Ever since the fox arrived, the rabbits have grown a bit scarce.) Not only that, but several days ago a wild turkey strolled past the lilacs.

In March and April, in the Northeast where I live, it is usually quite chilly. Even by late April the trees still retain their winter nakedness. While there are still no leaves, the birds build their nests and some begin to lay eggs, but they, like the trees, are waiting for warmer days.

In early June a great change occurs almost overnight. The birds know exactly the day of the change. As the weather warms, the tiny chicks, that have been all stretched-skin, greedy beak, and bone, sprout feathers and hop from branch to leafing branch. Only days before, this activity would have exposed them to great danger. Only after the leaves begin to unfold from their tight, sticky buds is it safe for the birds to leave the nest.

The garden briefly becomes a paradise. I tend to drop my work and wander "aimlessly" in that paradise. (There are advantages to being a self-

LETTER VIII

employed writer and movie director that outweigh the lack of medical coverage and a pension!) Often I forget to get dressed in the morning. If you were unkind enough to spy on me, you would see me in my bathrobe and in bare feet at all hours, creeping about, kneeling to smell, to breathe in the aroma of pure-white narcissus and peering between tangled thatches of bramble branches to count the mockingbird chicks.

The scents as well as the sights in the garden are paradisical. The incense of the lilacs soon replaces the fading scent of the early spring narcissus. The cold fragrance of the dew on the new grass and the smell of the mud on the tidal flats of the river waft on the morning breeze. The heavy earthy stench of the compost pile, as I break it open to dig the rich, rotten soil into my tomato patch, is overpowering. It is these smells, as well as the sights of the life in the garden, that make it a paradise. That is why I am sorry to be at my desk, writing! I am sorry because I am missing some moments in my garden that come but once a year. And I am sorry because there are not many springtimes in one lifetime.

Life is too short! We long for more. We long for not just any kind of life, but for life in the garden, life with creatures, life with the scent of lilacs in early June, life near a mother dove who will not leave her babies, no matter what. We long for a life of friendship with all the creatures of the world. (Surely this is why we love our pets so. What is more delightful than a beloved, loyal dog?)

It seems to me that we long for a rich organic life because it is the life that God created us for. We long to know why we are here, and part of that longing is expressed by our desire to draw closer to the creation around us. It seems to me that there is a reason for this. I believe we have were created to be gardener-priests. I believe that our true human task is to see with our inner eyes and to offer what we see to God from the depths of our beings. We were made because of love, and love of creation is part of the essence of our being.

Since nothing is perfect enough to offer the Creator, the only thing we

LETTER VIII

gardener-priests can do—whether ordained like you, Father, or whether lay priests like the rest of us—is to offer God to God. That is why we call the Eucharist a sacrifice. That is why we call it Communion. Through it we offer God to God. It seems to me that this communion is the reason for our creation.

It seems to me that the Eucharist is not the only bloodless sacrifice.

> *"Praise the Lord from the earth, ye dragons, and all deeps; fire, and hail; snow, and vapours; stormy wind, fulfilling his word; mountains, and all hills; fruitful trees, and all cedars; beasts, and all cattle; creeping things, and flying fowl; kings of the earth, and all people; princes, and all judges of the earth; both young men, and maidens; old men, and children: Let them praise the name of the Lord; for his name alone is excellent; his glory is above the earth and heaven. He also hath exalted the horn of His people."*
> *(Psalm 148: 7-14)*

The whole of creation is a bloodless sacrifice if we will truly see what is around and in us. Surely this is why Mt. Athos is called "the Panagia's garden." (A monk once told me that you can tell a lot about the spiritual condition of a monastery by how the monks keep their land and gardens.)

It appears that our relationship to the created world reflects a deeper reality about who we really are. There are many parts to reality, just as there are many parts to our being. There is our body and our soul and our spirit and our reason and our heart. There is also that innermost spiritual intellect that St. Maximos the Confessor said contains the kernel of immortality, the reflection of uncreated life in us—that is, the seed that falls into the ground to be raised incorruptible.

It seems that there are really two of us occupying the same space. We have our physical bodies and the seeds of our spiritual bodies within us, all at once. According to the Fathers, these elements are not in separate compartments but are mixed up in one substance we call a "person."

LETTER VIII

The reason there is more to each of us than our physical bodies is because we are a reflection of all of God's creation in Heaven and on earth. We have in us both the seen and unseen, the obvious and not so obvious, the physical and the spiritual.

As St. Maximos the Confessor writes:

> *"From created beings we come to know their Cause; from the differences between created beings we learn about the indwelling Wisdom of creation; and from the natural activity of created beings we discern the indwelling Life of creation, the power which gives created beings their life—the Holy Spirit."*
> *("First Century of Various Texts,"* The Philokalia, *vol. II, p. 180)*

So what does my garden and our spiritual bodies have to do with us all being gardener-priests? Just this: We are gardener-priests in the sense that we are "go-betweens," intermediaries between all the parts of creation in the same way that Christ, the God-Man, is the go-between between humanity and God the Father. And just as Christ offers each one of us back to the Father, the Holy Spirit, and Himself, so we "discern the indwelling Life of creation" and offer the world around us back to the Trinity.

The Fathers teach that we human beings alone are in a position to give the world its true meaning. We alone fulfill its existence. "Out of the ground the Lord God formed every beast of the field, and every fowl of the air; and brought them unto Adam to see what he would call them; and whatsoever Adam called each living creature, that was the name thereof" (Genesis 2:19).

When we love the world and see it for what it truly is—in other words, when we name it—we are doing our job, just like the mother dove is doing hers by sitting ever so still on her eggs. However, it seems that the difference between us and the mother dove is that she has been made by God

LETTER VIII

to fulfill her destiny whether she chooses to or not. But we are allowed to choose. This is a terrible responsibility. We can choose to learn from the High Priest, Christ, to be go-betweens, intermediaries between the spiritual world and the physical world, or we can choose to pretend that only the physical world exists, and that, for instance, math and science are the only true ways to describe reality.

I believe that sometimes we forget why we were made. And when we forget, we become discouraged. When we think that we were created for jobs, other than the task of offering back ourselves and creation to the Trinity, we become empty and discouraged. It seems to me that the only way out of such discouragement is to remember that we only have one task. It is to be the priests of creation. This is why the Scriptures tell us that we humans are higher than the angels. The Fathers say that it is because we alone dwell in both the spiritual and physical realm and alone are both spiritual and physical. As St. Maximos writes: "We learn about the indwelling Wisdom of creation." We contain both realms, the "natural activity of created beings" and "the power which gives created beings their life" in us.

Only we can fulfill creation by recognizing in it a sacred beauty, because only we, of all creatures on earth, are simultaneously part of creation and apart from it. We alone have the capacity to contemplate. It is this ability to stand apart that gives us the ability to name the creatures. But with this unique ability comes unique responsibility. If we no longer care about the birds and the smell of the narcissus, then who will? If we do not learn to understand what is truly real and beautiful and sacred in this life, how will we recognize it in the next? If we do not give spiritual meaning to the physical world, who will? If Adam will not name (in other words, contemplate and understand) the creatures, who will? The rape of our earth and our utilitarian approach to it are a terrible indication of just how apostate we have become and how long it has been since we fulfilled our priestly function.

LETTER VIII

This world is an archetype of another. What we know *here* that is good and beautiful and true, we will recognize in the spiritual world, which, by the way, is every bit as real as this world and a lot more "solid." The Fathers say it is made out of a much finer and delicate set of materials than is the present world. The Fathers say that these "materials" are so delicate that it is hard to see them with these eyes of flesh.

St. Maximos the Confessor writes:

> *"Every contemplative intellect that has 'the sword of the Spirit, which is the word of God' (Eph. 6:17) and that has cut off in itself the activity of the visible world, has attained virtue. When it has excised from itself the image of sensible appearances it finds the truth existing in the inner essences of created beings, which is the foundation of natural contemplation. And when it has transcended the being of created things, it will receive the illumination of the divine and unoriginate Unity who is the foundation of the mystery of true theology. God reveals Himself to each person according to each person's mode of conceiving Him. To those whose aspiration transcends the complex structure of matter, and whose psychic powers are fully integrated in a single unceasing gyration around God, He reveals Himself as Unity and Trinity. In this way He both shows forth His own existence and mystically makes known the mode in which that existence subsists."*
>
> *("First Century of Various Texts, 94-95," The Philokalia, vol. II, p. 186)*

To some it is briefly given to truly see. For instance, at the Transfiguration on Mt. Tabor, the Fathers tell us that Christ was not transfigured at all. It was the Apostles who were transfigured! They were briefly enabled by Christ to see Him as He always is.

> *"Christ, Who was transfigured on Mount Tabor, is not only perfect God but also perfect Man. He was transfigured in His human nature—it was His human body which shone with the uncreated Light of Divinity. But the human nature which He took and united*

LETTER VIII

to the Divine Nature belongs to us also. Christ assumed our nature and transfigured it. The assumption of our human nature by the Logos effected healing—the transformation of this nature. St. Gregory Palamas tells us that this transformation, deification, and transfiguration of human nature was accomplished from the moment Christ assumed our human nature. . . . Thus, the Transfiguration is the revelation of the deified human nature of Christ which is potentially appropriated by all who share in the nature. . . . This includes you and me—what an astonishing, wonderful truth!

The Incarnate Christ, Who shone with divine glory on the mountain, is God, never-changing, and so He remains the same today as He was on Mount Tabor. He is God, the same then, the same now. He revealed Himself to His disciples then and continues to reveal Himself to His disciples now. Our loving God comes to reveal to us, through Christ, the light of true divinity—the gift of grace. Christ fulfills the Old Covenant as told by the prophets—the healing of our humanity. Let us with joy follow long and faithfully as did the apostles. Through fasting, vigil and prayer let us ascend our Mount Tabor by the path of ascetism. Let us prepare our hearts and souls for Christ's Transfiguration. Let us join each other to give thanks to God and to praise His infinite love and wisdom. Let us joyfully celebrate this marvelous Feast of the Transfiguration together—one heart, one mind, one body in Christ to the glory of God forever and ever. Amen."
(Life Transfigured, vol. 27/2, Summer, 1995)

The uncreated light that fills Christ is not turned on and off, but our ability to perceive the true reality of things as they are is highly inconsistent. God, however, is always God. His creation is full of His presence, whether we are willfully blind to it or not. The Holy Spirit animates even those who deny His existence. It is *we* who live in a state of illusion. Reality does not change. God does not change.

LETTER VIII

God does not despise our world or our physical condition. We know this since the Holy Spirit condescended to reveal Himself in the form of a dove. God the Father knows when each sparrow falls. The God-Man, Christ, chose a human mother as the way to come to us in His Incarnation (that He could build a bridge back to God the Father by becoming a man, in order that we might become gods, true sons by adoption in imitation of the uncreated Son). Christ used physical miracles—water, wine, bread, oil, a donkey, fish, and honeycomb to manifest His two natures. He condescended to let the weeping women bathe His crucified body, wrap Him in linen, and perfume Him with myrrh. The mother dove, even in our world in which people sin, still praises God with each moment she sits patiently on her nest. God has not only created, He is recreating the world in an irreversible process that began in the Theotokos' womb. God does not despise the small things He has made. He has used His creation to save it. So let us not despise our priestly calling to name the creatures and fulfill creation.

Let us remember that it is only because of sin that we do not always *see* reality for what it is with our spiritual eyes. And let us remember that when we do not see, our blindness causes discouragement.

It is the sights, smells, and the feel of things in our hands and under our feet that brings up the most vital question about our true nature. The question is one of perception, of how we finally see the world about us.

Fr. Aristotle, don't you ever sense that there is another *you* looking out through your fleshly eyes? Don't you ever feel that there is someone deep under your skin, who hears through your ears and touches with your hands and smells through your nose? And don't you ever think that there is someone in you, in you deeper than your brain, inside all of you—not just your head and mind—that hears your thoughts and tells you what they mean?

It is with our immortal inner eyes—with our spiritual intellect—that we look out on the world. We can truly see only if we will work to train ourselves through ascetic struggle.

LETTER VIII

St. Thalassios writes:

"The more the [spiritual] intellect is purified, the more the soul is granted spiritual knowledge of divine principles. He who has disciplined his body and dwells in a state of spiritual knowledge finds that through this knowledge he is purified still further."
("Fourth Century on Love, Self-control and Life in accordance with the Intellect, 77-78," The Philokalia, vol. II, p. 330)

But much of the time we do not allow our immortal inner person to see and hear and touch the real world though our mortal flesh. We are too busy, noisy, crude, and brutal to hear the still, small voice that is in us and all around us. We are too distracted to discipline our bodies and dwell "in a state of spiritual knowledge." We are too undisciplined to quiet our passions long enough for true contemplation. That is why we must remind ourselves and each other over and over again why God has made us to be here on earth. And that is why silence, contemplation, and prayer are the only true necessities of life. In contemplation of God, His creation, and ourselves we may offer up the sacrifice of thanksgiving in order that we may fulfill our one and only task.

As ever,
Frank

LETTER IX

Dear Fr. Aristotle,

In your last letter you told me the story of the young man, George. I am so sorry for you as his priest and for his mother and father. What a tragedy it is when Orthodox young people leave the Church to join one of the thousands of Protestant sects that dot our blighted landscape!

You ask me for my opinion on why so many Orthodox seem to have "lost their children." I presume you are referring to the fact that many second and third generation ethnic Orthodox do not seem to share their parents', let alone their grandparents', piety and commitment to the Church.

I have certainly noticed what might be called a missing generation of Orthodox. It often seems that congregations are predominantly filled with elderly people and some young families. Often the young families are there "for the children," but the parents do not seem particularly devout. It seems that when the children grow older, the parents often stop coming to church. Thankfully there are many exceptions to this trend. Many communities are vibrant, growing, and full of people of all ages as well as many converts. However, the problems you mention are all too real.

An entire generation of professional people ages twenty-five to fifty-five seem to be missing from some of our Orthodox communities. Of course this is a drastic generalization, but my own very unscientific "study," made while visiting and speaking at eighty or ninety or so parishes of all jurisdictions seems to bear out this observation. After I speak, often some mother, father, grandfather, or grandmother will come up to me and say, "I wish my son (or daughter) could have heard you, but he (or she) refuses to come to anything at the church now."

As to why there are so many Orthodox who seem to lose interest in the life of the Church, of course there is no simple answer. Obviously at the heart of this problem is a spiritual battle beyond human explanation. Nor is this loss of faith confined to the Orthodox. Protestants, Roman Catholics, and Jews have all suffered from attrition as well. Nevertheless,

LETTER IX

here are a few personal observations, largely drawn from my own conversations with grandparents, parents, young people, priests, monks, and bishops across North America.

Let us remember that we live in a very secular culture. This is true, even though it is also a very "religious" culture. However, from the Orthodox point of view, the various religions of North America—for instance, modern Protestantism and post-Vatican II "user-friendly" Roman Catholicism—are themselves now very secularized when compared to Orthodoxy. For instance, post-Vatican II Roman Catholics do not fast for an extended period of time before Communion. Most Protestants do not even know what Lent is, let alone how to keep it as Christians. I know!

Not that long ago I considered myself very "religious," and yet I lived a completely irreligious life as measured by any historical, patristic, Christian standard of practice. As a Protestant, the idea of ascetic struggle, an idea that has been at the heart of Christian spirituality for two thousand years, was completely foreign to me. I would have had no understanding whatsoever of what St. Thalassios, or any of the desert Fathers, were writing about or why the need to struggle against the passions is indispensable in the journey to salvation.

St. Thalassios writes:

> *"Ascetic struggle—fasting, vigils, patience, forbearance—produces a clear conscience. He who patiently endures unsought trials becomes humble, full of hope and spiritually mature."*
> (*"Third Century On Love, Self-control and Life . . . 14-15,"* The Philokalia, *vol. II, p. 321-22)*

The Orthodox idea of ascetic struggle as the road to salvation is almost completely foreign to all Western Christians. This has been the case in Protestant circles for over four hundred years. An antimonastic, anti-ascetic attitude has been part of the Protestant *ethos* from the time of

LETTER IX

Martin Luther. And in Roman Catholic circles since the 1960s, this anti-monastic attitude has been growing also. Nevertheless, many Orthodox seem unaware of how vast the gulf is that separates Orthodoxy from the Western religions of today. Indeed, we have failed to grasp the fact that, from an Orthodox point of view, even the religious elements of our society are, in fact, secular. Indeed, when I refer to the "secular culture" or "secularism," it seems that these terms accurately describe both the overtly secular parts of our society and most of the religious ones as well.

Apparently the Orthodox faithful who emigrated to North America had a vague notion that America was a "Christian country" and that, while the rubrics of Orthodox worship were superficially different from those of Protestantism and Catholicism, the values, teaching, and practices were the same as those of the Orthodox. It seems to me that nothing could be further from the truth. Orthodox naiveté about the North American culture into which we brought our families has cost us dearly. It has cost many of us our children.

On a Greek island or in a traditional Palestinian, Ethiopian, or Russian village, society and religion were once mutually supporting. The necessity to instruct, explain, defend, and train up one's children in the Orthodox way *against* the surrounding society was not of paramount concern since Church and society shared the same beliefs and taboos. Of course there were exceptions to this rule in Orthodox history. In both Russia and Greece, imported Western humanism began to influence some Orthodox, especially from the eighteenth century onward. But usually priest, teacher, and neighbor were the friend of the Orthodox villager's moral values and religious aspirations. Society was a prop and support for the Orthodox parents' worldview. The need to defend one's family against foreign philosophies was itself a foreign idea. Even under the Turks Greek village life often had a normal (i.e. traditional) Orthodox quality to it.

In the "old country," the Orthodox faithful expected that if they went to church, prayed, worked, and lived according to the Orthodox ascetic rule of prayer, fasting, and self-discipline, their children would follow in their

LETTER IX

footsteps. A grandchild would keep Lent, go to Communion, and pray at his grandmother's side. A son would join his father in church for Vespers. The Church calendar taught the Christian faith. The national holidays were the feasts of the Church. Someone who preached a contrary vision of life, such as sexual liberation, atheism, or moral relativism, would have been driven from the village. The life of the Church and the life of the culture were one and the same.

The situation changed radically when the Orthodox emigrated to North America. They were no longer living in a mutually supporting society. They became spiritual refugees. Whether they knew it or not, they were surrounded by a culture hostile to the Orthodox way of life. Soon this culture would begin to obliterate Orthodox faith in the hearts of second- and third-generation Orthodox.

Today our North American schools, particularly our universities, teach the exact opposite of what we Orthodox believe to be true. The secular worldview is exclusively taught on a whole range of topics, from psychology, sociology, and literary studies to sexual morality and the ultimate meaning of life.

While maintaining its outward friendliness and commitment to pluralism, our society is not on the side of the traditional Orthodox parent. In fact, the *ethos* of North America is dramatically opposed to the Orthodox parents' deepest beliefs. The veneer of tolerance and pluralism merely covers up a Rousseau-Thoreauian humanistic-Enlightenment hostility to traditional religion and, above all, to traditional lifestyles.

America touts itself as an egalitarian society. We Orthodox believe in a hierarchy that begins on earth and stretches to the throne of God. America is profoundly materialistic and consumeristic. We Orthodox believe that self-denial and ascetic struggle is essential for salvation. In stark contrast to the Orthodox idea of moral absolutes, the only absolute in modern America is that there are no moral absolutes, let alone absolute non-negotiable truths. One is free to believe anything personally, as long

LETTER IX

as one does not commit the *faux pas* of saying it is true in an absolute or binding way that excludes falsehood or that would brand another philosophy as wrong. The very word *orthodox* is un-American. There are no orthodoxies in America, no right ways of doing things or believing. This relativistic worldview places the Orthodox, whether we acknowledge it or not, on a collision course with secular and most "religious" American society.

The sad irony is that the very desire to "arrive" and to "make it," for the sake of their children, expressed by the hard work of the first generation of Orthodox immigrants, often has cost them their children. The ambition to give our children "the chance we never had," the desire to see our children have a "good education," is at least part of the reason that so many Orthodox families have lost our children to secular society and to American-style Protestant sects.

Bishop Isaiah of Denver (Greek Orthodox) writes:

> *"The bold materialism permeating many of our people's lives may be traced to a number of the first immigrants.*
>
> *They were the highest example of what it means for one to sacrifice. However, because they did not want their children to undergo the same hardships and sufferings they endured, they taught them to gather, but not how to give.*
>
> *Most Greek Orthodox people [in America] today have never had to sacrifice because of the abnormal protection of their parents and grandparents."*
> *("The Second Coming of Christ and Our Quest for Success,"* The Orthodox Observer, *September, 1995)*

Besides simply spoiling our children with overindulgence, it seems to me that the tragedy of the loss of our children occurred for two other reasons. First, the Orthodox underestimated the power and attraction of anti-

LETTER IX

traditional, antihierarchical, secular propaganda. (This virulent propaganda has been part and parcel of the North American Protestant-Humanistic educational system since the late nineteenth century.) Second, having misunderstood North America, we Orthodox failed to equip our children intellectually to withstand the secular onslaught. We have sent our children out into the world no more spiritually and intellectually prepared than they would have been back in the old country two hundred years ago. But the environment is radically different than the old country of two centuries ago, so the results have often been disastrous.

Many traditionalist Protestant and Roman Catholic parents have also made the mistake of underestimating the corrosive power of pluralistic secular America. Life in a small English or Sicilian village was no better preparation for surviving the New Babylon—North America—than life on Crete or Patmos. However, there is one *big difference* between the Orthodox and most other religiously believing emigrants to North America. The difference is the availability of support systems.

The Protestant emigrant is raising children in a subculture that, to the extent that it is still religious at all, is supportive of Protestant-style religion. For instance, the Protestant parent is living and raising his children in an environment in which many evangelistic ministries, such as the Billy Graham crusades, publishing companies, and various Protestant schools, help to provide respite from the pervasive secularism of our Knowledge Class—our cultural elite, media, and educators. The Roman Catholic parent also has help. This help has come through a network of parochial schools. Until the post-Vatican II self-immolation of the American Roman Catholic Church in the 1960s and 1970s, these schools were quite religious in character.

The Orthodox parent receives scant help in preparing his children for the rigors of worldly life from his own church, let alone from the Roman Catholic or Protestant subcultures. The prevailing religious Western subculture, to the extent that its members are even aware of us, is as hostile to Orthodox Christianity as it is to pure humanistic secularism.

LETTER IX

Mormonism, Protestantism (all varieties), post-Vatican II Roman Catholicism, and the other Western religions do us precious little good. Indeed, the multicultural, multidenominational pluralism of North America simply makes it harder to pass on the Orthodox Tradition. Why fast when there are "many ways" to God? Why struggle when all you have to do is "accept Jesus into your heart"?

The Orthodox young person faces not only the subtle—or not so subtle—hostility of his or her secularized, and often atheistic, college professors and high school teachers, but also a host of fervent Protestant believers who doubt the quality of his or her salvation. The Orthodox young person is often assaulted by the Protestant fundamentalist asking questions such as, "Have you accepted Jesus as your personal savior?" or "Why do you have all those outward forms of worship? Don't you know this is idolatry?"

From the modernized Roman Catholic, the Orthodox young person hears comments like, "We're historic and liturgical, but we don't have to keep all those old-fashioned rules about fasting anymore! Why do you have to do all that stuff? It must be terribly hard to be Orthodox!" Or, "How come you're so closed? Our priest will let you receive Communion in our church if you want to take it. We welcome *everyone*! How come your priest won't let us receive in *your* church?"

I believe there are good answers to all these questions, just as there are good answers to the secular challenge to our faith. But the Orthodox believer may not know what those answers are. Nor may the believer know how bankrupt both Roman Catholic and Protestant Western theology, faith, and practice has become, or that many disillusioned Protestants and Roman Catholics are seeking the spiritual treasures that have been uniquely preserved in Orthodoxy. Perhaps one reason that so many Orthodox young people do not know this is that some of the Orthodox priests and bishops who lead them also seem oblivious to the spiritual hunger around them.

LETTER IX

Perhaps Orthodox ignorance of the surrounding culture has been compounded by an Orthodox leadership that has been somewhat corrupted by its long association with ecumenism. It seems that our Orthodox leaders have not always stood up and clearly addressed the issues of the day. They have not always taught what the fundamental differences are between Orthodox Christianity and Western heresy. Perhaps they have not spoken out because they do not wish to offend other Christians. But if bishops and priests refuse to teach, who will lead the people? How can the leadership expect the faithful to understand the differences between Orthodoxy and Protestantism or Roman Catholicism or secularism if they are seen in fraternal dialogue with the non-Orthodox on the one hand, and on the other never seem to draw a clear line between Orthodoxy and heterodoxy?

Too often the Orthodox have been taught, by example if not by word, that "being accepted" or "making it" in America is life's only real priority. What Orthodox immigrant, bent on success, is going to speak up, or alienate "the Americans," whether these are fellow students, clients, friends, educators, proselytizing Protestant neighbors, or modern Roman Catholics, if the price is going to be paid in the currency of one's worldly achievements? Who wants to risk the family business for the sake of Orthodox Truth when even some priests and bishops are silent?

Another thing that Orthodox immigrants were hardly prepared for, through no fault of their own, is the fact that in the West not all "Christians" are believers. Naturally we cannot judge the state of any individual's soul, but the triumph of secularism within Western religious bodies is a clear fact. In fact, many Western "Christians" are secularists in religious garb. In other words, the Orthodox had no concept of what we call liberal Protestantism or liberal, modern Roman Catholicism.

Orthodox ignorance of liberal Christianity is understandable. There was no equivalent of Aristotelian-Augustinian rationalism within the Eastern Church. Except when it was imported from the West, humanistic rationalism was foreign to Orthodoxy. But in the West things developed differently than in the East. From the thirteenth century on, with the rise of the

LETTER IX

Aristotelian-Scholastic movement, the Christianity of the West evolved into an altogether different religion from the Christianity of the East. Nor was there a reformation—or more accurately, a rebellion—in the Orthodox Church comparable to the Protestant Reformation. Nor did the so-called higher critical methods of biblical study invade the Orthodox Church as they did the Western churches by degrees from the nineteenth century onward (although we see signs of it creeping into our seminaries now).

The Orthodox emigrant had little experience with liberal Protestant and Roman Catholic churches that are not religious, pastors who have no faith, theologians who are in fact philosophers, or a spirituality that asks only that you feel fulfilled. It seems that the Orthodox drew false comfort and a false sense of security from the fact that there were so many churches and apparently religious people in America. What they did not realize was that North American religion is often empty, and that where it bears a theological resemblance to Orthodoxy, it nevertheless is completely dissimilar when it comes to the idea of how to achieve salvation. In fact, the idea of divinization is so foreign to Western Christians that to them this belief is a "proof" of Orthodoxy's "cultic" status!

What the Orthodox immigrants did not realize was that they had arrived in a new, declining "Roman empire" full of pagan religions, some of which were masquerading as traditional Christianity, but none of which had any resemblance to the Orthodox way of being, let alone to the Orthodox ideal of ascetic spiritual struggle to achieve divinization. It seems to me that the Orthodox faithful naively walked into a cultural battle for their children's souls with little or no understanding of the protagonists which were and are roughly divided into three groups:

(1) Conservative Roman Catholics and Protestants

(2) Liberal Roman Catholics and Protestants

(3) Antireligious secularists.

LETTER IX

The Orthodox faithful failed to realize that not one of these categories was friendly to Orthodoxy or even necessarily aware of it. (This is not to say that on an individual level some Americans were not sympathetic to individual Orthodox.)

The Orthodox mistakenly understood official tolerance as neutrality. For instance, they erroneously interpreted the official liberal Protestant commitment to ecumenism as a desire to learn about the Truth in order to be enlightened by it. In fact, it seems that this ecumenical tolerance was no more than a desire on the part of the Protestants to prove how "open-minded" and "pluralistic" they were. There was, of course, room for the Orthodox at the relativistic, ecumenical banquet. However, at this banquet all truth claims had to be laid aside as the entrance fee to participate in the feast of intellectual respectability. There was no room for the changeless Holy Tradition or the changeless Christ to Whom this Tradition bears witness.

The Orthodox learned too late that North Americans are not neutral to Orthodoxy. To the extent that they are aware of its ascetic call to holiness and its monastic tradition of self-denial in order to curb the passions, they are hostile to it. Indeed, the very "weirdness" of Orthodoxy in the eyes of "mainstream America" has been reason enough to further increase the sense of ethnic inferiority on the part of some Orthodox and their desire to "keep quiet and work hard" to "fit in" and to "make it."

The desire to hide one's Orthodox identity—to not appear different or odd to "the Americans"—has resulted in some Orthodox not keeping to our calendar of fasts and feasts, ascetic struggle, and prayer. It has also resulted in the Orthodox involving themselves in the dead end of ecumenical dialogue instead of concentrating on true missionary work. This has had a deadening effect on the Orthodox witness. The ecumenist goal is not to make converts or to see the Orthodox Church grow, but to make friends. The ecumenist goal is *unity,* not salvation; world *peace,* not holiness.

The desire to be liked has resulted in the Orthodox keeping perversely

LETTER IX

quiet at the outrages perpetrated by our fellow members of the World and National Council of Churches, to which we Orthodox presently belong. It seems to me that one compromise has led to another. Silence has become cowardice. The Orthodox witness has evaporated in a haze of insubstantial good feeling and self-congratulation. We "belong," but perhaps we are no longer as sure of who we are.

It is clear that the Orthodox reticence to evangelize has cost us dearly. It has not only cost us in the practical area of growth, but it has cost us spiritually as well. We have denied one of the central tenets of Holy Tradition. We have turned our back on carrying out the Great Commission.

St. Maximos the Confessor writes:

> *"A person who through the grace of God partakes of divine blessings is under an obligation to share them ungrudgingly with others. For Scripture says, 'Freely you have received, freely give' (Matt. 10:8). He who hides the gift in the earth accuses the Lord of being hard-hearted and mean (cf. Matt. 25:24) and in order to spare the flesh he pretends to know nothing about holiness; while he who sells the truth to enemies, and is then revealed as avid for self-glory, hangs himself, unable to bear the disgrace (cf. Matt 26:15, 27:5).* ("First Century on Theology, 29,"* The Philokalia, *vol. II, p. 119-20)*

Our Orthodox reticence to stand up and be counted, as we have pretended to "know nothing about holiness," has eroded Orthodox parents' ability to inculcate the faith of the Fathers into their children. A retiring, silent witness is no witness. Bishops and priests more interested in being accepted through "ecumenical dialogue" than in holiness of life and Orthodox missionary work have let their young people down. Silence in the face of falsehood is no virtue. St. Maximos calls this silence "selling the truth to our enemies." The fruit of ecumenism bears witness to the fail-

LETTER IX

ure of the Orthodox ecumenical effort. How many converts have the ecumenists made amongst the heterodox in the last sixty years? How many
evangelistic efforts have they mounted to reach Protestants, Roman
Catholics, and others with Orthodoxy? The answer to both questions is
"None" (or hardly any). In fact, some ecumenists are overtly hostile to
evangelistic efforts made by their fellow Orthodox. They seem to find
evangelism embarrassing and inconvenient. To them it gets in the way of
the "ecumenical dialogue" they are conducting. They tend to regard the
West as "Christian," therefore "off limits" to evangelism.

Not long ago I was at an Orthodox conference on evangelism at which
an Orthodox bishop from Europe, who works full-time with the World
Council of Churches, actually stood up and said that he thought Orthodox
evangelistic efforts in Western "Christian" countries like the United States
should cease. Of course his basic assumption that America *is* a Christian
nation was unsubstantiated as was his premise that evangelism should be
left in the hands of the paid, professional ecumenical bureaucrats such as
himself.

There are many examples of the price we have paid by not speaking
boldly. The evangelistic silence of the Orthodox has been contagious. It
has had the effect of creating a climate of silence and a fear of speaking
out boldly. This has gone well beyond evangelism and has now affected
the ability of the leaders of the Church to teach their own.

The Orthodox young woman who has never heard her priest and bishop courageously denounce the murder of unborn children can blame *them*
for the sin of her abortion. And the Orthodox young man who has heard
his ecumenist priest, bishop, or hierarch say, "We are to be reunited with
Rome," or, "We are really all Christian," can scarcely be blamed if he ceas-
es to fast, go to confession, or keep the Orthodox rule of prayer.

We teach by example. An entire generation of Orthodox does not know
that evangelism is an important part of the Orthodox Holy Tradition. They
have not seen their priests and bishops evangelizing North American

LETTER IX

Protestants, Jews, atheists, humanists, and Roman Catholics. In fact, the word *proselytize* has become a dirty word and has somehow been confused with the word *evangelize*. No wonder many Orthodox are confused as to the truth claims of our faith. If it is not worth sharing, why is it worth keeping? If it is only to be talked about in ecumenical dialogue, as if a middle ground between Truth and falsehood exists, then how can it be true in the sense that it is worth struggling for?

The lack of evangelistic zeal has been contagious. The fact that an entire generation of Orthodox were raised by parents who rarely, if ever, tried to convert the non-Orthodox has a lot to do with the fact that they also did not go to confession, rarely received the Eucharist, treated parish business like old country politics, and often gave grudgingly to their churches.

Children who grow up in homes where money, education, "getting ahead," "being accepted," "fitting in," and "making it" are venerated or even worshiped will do the same themselves, whatever lip service their priest and parents pay to the Church and however many icons hang in the kitchen. And if a young person's priest and parents have failed to grasp the true nature of the place in which they live and what it will do to their parishioners and children, then there is little reason to expect that the second generation of Orthodox will remain Orthodox.

As ever,
Frank

LETTER X

Dear Fr. Aristotle,

I have been thinking about your comment that my last letter was "incomplete" because I never outlined the particulars of the "American situation that the immigrants faced." Here are some further thoughts.

Perhaps due to the fact that many Orthodox arrived in America both poor and fleeing persecution gave them a tremendous sense of gratitude to the North American society that received them. This gratitude was, of course, not wholly misplaced. But perhaps it eroded the Orthodox faithful's willingness to look clearly and unsentimentally at the society around them. Had they taken a hard look, this is what they would have seen:

(1) America is not a Christian culture;

(2) modern American culture is based on a mixture of Western, humanistic, modern Roman Catholic, Protestant, liberal Protestant, and Enlightenment ideas;

(3) all the elements of American society agree on one thing: sacramentality, hierarchy, tradition, and asceticism are "out"; pluralism, relativism, egalitarianism, democracy, self-realization, progress, and individualism are "in";

(4) in the sense that the "scientific method" has deeply stirred the American imagination, America—with the possible exception of the late Soviet Union—is the most materialistic culture the world has ever produced . Faith in evolutionary "progress" is now almost absolute. The words *new, improved, progressive,* and *open-minded* might as well be our secular beatitudes;

(5) most Orthodox immigrants from the 1920s to the 1960s arrived in America while the nation's elite, the Knowledge Class, was in a period of historic transition from Protestant-religious-humanistic belief to a purely humanistic secular "liberal" philosophy. This philosophy soon began to

LETTER X

express itself in outright hostility to all traditional religion;

(6) the ideals America was founded on were derived from the Aristotelian-Enlightenment-Western philosophical worldview. This worldview is the opposite of Eastern Orthodox belief in mystery and salvation through ascetic struggle, let alone our belief in the possibility of divinization;

(7) the very concept of Holy Mystery, ascetic life, and a hierarchy of archetypal meaning (that gives meaning and order to reality), let alone monastic contemplation, does not exist in American or in most of post-Enlightenment Western European culture, of which America is a half-baked derivative;

(8) the American landscape is dotted with churches but not monasteries. This is an unintentional visual reminder of American hostility to Orthodox ideas of spiritual and ascetic struggle. The American "God" loves you and has a wonderful plan for your life, but he does not want you to have to struggle to realize it;

(9) in American churches, a variety of religions are taught—"feel-good" materialism, Augustinian Calvinism, "touchy-feely" liberal post-Vatican II Roman Catholicism, Protestant "psychobabble," New Age eco-earth worship, atheism, piecemeal "liturgical-style worship," social collectivism, "charismatic" faith (in other words, group psychosis), higher critical biblical studies—but any illusion that somehow this fever-swamp of abundant religiosity is equivalent to the many Orthodox monasteries of Greece, the Middle East, and Russia is just that, an illusion. It is the illusion of religion without ascetic, life-changing struggle. It is the illusion of the crucifixion without nails, of salvation through self-realization, of worship as entertainment. It is a "people's democratic religion," not the faith of the Fathers believed by all Orthodox Christians everywhere since the beginning; and

(10) the American landscape is dotted with educational institutions, most of which have some sort of historical Roman Catholic or Protestant affiliation. But the life within these schools and the monolithic atheist worldview

LETTER X

taught in them is now unremittingly antagonistic to all traditional religious worldviews.

It seems that the Greek, Russian, Arab, or African Orthodox Christian who thought that in coming to America he had escaped persecution and barbarism forever had no idea of the level of intolerance toward traditional religious ideas that would confront his children. He may have escaped the Turk or the KGB, but he had merely traded overt brutality for covert hostility to the Faith of his Fathers. He had exchanged persecution for seduction. He had been fooled by the beautiful veneer and had failed to comprehend what lay under the surface. He could now choose where his son or daughter went to university, but what he did not realize was that wherever they went to school, they would be taught the same materialistic philosophy that had been preached by Marx and Lenin. The only difference was that the professor would wear a tweed jacket rather than jack boots, and that he or she would not have Orthodox students shot but merely give them an "F" on their sociology paper if they did not "broaden their outlook."

As ever,
Frank

LETTER XI

Dear Fr. Aristotle,

You justly rebuke me in your letter for making it sound as if I blamed the older generation of Orthodox for the loss of their children. In talking about why some Orthodox have lost their children to the secular culture, it may seem as if I am laying the blame all at the parents', or priests' and bishops', door. This is not so.

The Orthodox who have been enticed away from the Church bear a heavy responsibility for their own choice. They certainly cannot blame their parents or priest. No home or parish is perfect, yet the Church calls us all to transcend the limits of our background and choose to follow Christ. We are all responsible for our actions.

Tragically, the Orthodox young people who have left the Church for a so-called secular life have made a very bad bargain. They have left the greatest treasure and storehouse of meaning and beauty in the world for a spiritually failed and esthetically bankrupt secularism. This secularism is imploding. From the collapse of the Communist regime in Russia to the declining educational system in American secularism, it is disintegrating before our very eyes.

The overly ambitious young person who is now "too busy" for the Orthodox Church and in favor of "making it" in the so-called fast lane of secular society shows bad judgment. The Orthodox who have abandoned the Church in favor of the secular West have left dry land for the "safety" of a berth on the Titanic. One who can walk away from the Church in favor of our dying, secular, humanistic culture is to be pitied above all men. He has exchanged living water for putrid sewage.

The secularized Orthodox is not the only tragically misguided person. The formerly Orthodox man or woman who joins one of the thousands of Protestant denominations or "born-again" sects in hopes of finding a deeper spiritual experience exhibits the same intellectual and spiritual bankruptcy as the person who abandons the Orthodox Church for secularism.

LETTER XI

A person who abandons the Church of the ages for a more trendy, modern, or even fun "Christianity" reminds me of someone too slothful or timid to go to Europe who goes to Disney's Epcot Center instead! It is, they say, "easier, and you get to see a lot of European stuff all in one place." But there is a problem. Epcot is a fake. It is a plastic, predigested, trivialized "Europe". It may be easier, more fun, nicer, and even more meaningful to some, but it is not the real thing.

Easy, one-stop, mass-produced Protestant and modern Roman Catholic religion that requires no more than you feel good about yourself is also a fake. It is as fraudulent as the French Quarter of Disneyland.

There is a profound difference between the authentic and inauthentic in any area of life. Even when the authentic is spoiled or imperfect, it is still authentic. Even when the inauthentic is in good condition, it is still inauthentic. A damaged Fabergé egg is still a lot more valuable than a perfect replica.

The tragically deluded men and women who wander away from the Orthodox Church in search of a more emotionally satisfying and lively Christianity or easy material and spiritual self-realization have unwittingly sold their souls for a counterfeit. And the excuse that the Orthodox Church is far from perfect or does not "meet my needs" is no excuse at all. Moreover, what they have done is only possible for one generation to do. The lapsed Orthodox will not have any stability in their lives comparable to the stability they were given. It is one thing to be raised in the Orthodox Church and to walk away in possession of the spiritual and esthetic memories that give one's life a sacramental shape. It is another to have no memories of sacramental religious meaning and beauty and to have only the emptiness modern America offers the wandering soul.

Assuredly, the Orthodox young person or adult who drifts away from the faith is living in a state of delusion. Their delusion is that their secular, Protestant, or modern Roman Catholic life is going to work. What they do not realize is that it will work only by inertia. It will work only for a time. In other words, the sheer depth of the spiritual roots they have, even long

78

LETTER XI

after they have been wrenched from their source, will still provide a sense of sacred meaning to their lives. However, this spiritual legacy will eventually run dry. Moreover, their children will begin their spiritual journeys where they end theirs. This same principle is also at work in our secular society. It draws on past art, music, literature, and ideas of civility that could never have been produced by post-Enlightenment, modern, nihilistic philosophy. The secular person who listens to Bach and reads Dante is cheating. They say they are secular, but they keep their sanity through enjoying the piety of others and the artistic beauty produced by a deep sense of the sacred.

The children of the lapsed Orthodox will never possess or pass on the reserves of meaning and beauty their parents had to draw on. Theirs will be lives of failed marriages, wasted time, superficial relationships, and the noise and clutter so typical of the modern age. And even if this is not so for them, it will be for their rootless, Americanized children and grandchildren.

The lapsed Orthodox take what is good from their Church, culture, and parents, but refuse to hand it on to their own children. Their lives were given meaning by their grandmother's prayers, their mother's selfless hard work, their father's simple piety, yet they will never provide these strengths or memories to their own children and grandchildren. The lapsed are truly desert valleys that soak up the water of life but refuse to let others taste it. They live on the borrowed currency of the sweet memories of incense. The taste of the Eucharist lingers on their lips. The scent of basil stirs echoes of blessings far off. The sound of a bell, the sight of a bearded figure in a *rason*, the flavor of a certain kind of sweet their grandmother once baked, the smoke from a charcoal grill, the dark interior of an ancient, white church on a sunny hill, a faded icon in a corner—all these things evoke a certain memory, a certain longing, a stirring of their conscience. But they refuse to listen to the still, small voice of God. As a result, their children and children's children will never know the Truth.

And what have the lapsed, Westernized, Romanized, secularized, or Protestantized Orthodox traded our irreplaceable and priceless heritage

LETTER XI

for? Badly written, cheaply produced, Sunday morning television! "People's Masses!" Meaningless careers as "successful" lawyers, doctors, secretaries, and businessmen! They have become women too busy to go to church, keep the fasts, or pray before the icons their grandmothers left them. They have become men who refuse to repair the churches their fathers built with their bare hands. They have married non-Orthodox spouses and condemned their children to lives of religious and moral uncertainty. They have abandoned a two-thousand-year-old religious tradition in favor of "making it" in a two-hundred-year-old failed experiment in selfishness we call "America."

Ironically, the lapsed Orthodox have betrayed their Church, their families, and their culture at the very hour the humanistic-secular-Protestant society they are so eager to join is in moral despair. The secular society is looking for the exact kind of meaning that we Orthodox have always possessed. What do you think the New Age movement is if not a desperate search for spiritual meaning in the spiritual desert created by faith in reason and science? What do you think the Protestant and Roman Catholic "charismatic movement" is if not a frantic, misguided attempt to rediscover the mystical, sacramental aspect of worship the Roman Catholics destroyed after Vatican II and the Protestants abandoned centuries earlier? What do you think all the self-help and so-called codependency groups are if not a sad counterfeit of religious community life? What do you think psychological counseling is if not a pitiful imitation of confession to a priest? Why do you think millions of bewildered and unhappy secularists go to Billy Graham crusades if not to find the sacred meaning of life? Why do you think thousands of disillusioned feminists are quitting their jobs, having babies, and fighting to stay home with their children, if not to try and rediscover their own deepest human roots?

The secular culture of the West, produced by the Roman Catholic Church, the Reformation, and the Enlightenment, has failed. Millions of people in the West are now looking for spiritual, sacramental, and human meaning. Specifically, they long for mystical, religious meaning in their lives. They

LETTER XI

long for a return to the sacred. The problem is that it is easier to seek meaning than to find the Truth. Once the historic bonds with Truth have been severed, it is hard to reestablish them. (Ask any traditionalist Roman Catholic. Ask any traditionalist Episcopalian.) Once we have taken ourselves off the narrow path, it is hard to remember where it is.

Salvation is a journey requiring self-discipline. Self-discipline is a habit of life. It is not learned in a book. It is not picked up casually. It takes generations to inculcate the good habits of prayer, fasting, and ascetic struggle necessary to find the narrow path of salvation.

We are not saved as individuals only, but as part of a community of faith called the Orthodox Church. We are baptized into the Church, not into egocentric isolation. We come as the people of God to God, not as individuals. We participate in the changeless sacramental tradition with others. The community of Orthodox faith is made up of communities we call families. These families create a culture of faith. Once the ancient bonds are cut, or one generation abandons its duty to pass on the light it was given, the community of faith can die out in one particular place or another almost overnight. As the extreme secularity of Protestant northern Europe proves, we are always only one generation away from the darkness of spiritual ignorance. As the chaos of the post-Vatican II Roman Catholic Church proves, we are only one step away from innovationist folly destroying all we hold sacred.

The repentant, lapsed Orthodox who suddenly wishes to return to the fold may have a nasty surprise. The fold may not be there. We always imagine that someone else will keep things going, even if we do not. "Mom will make my bed and fix dinner, even if I stay out playing with my friends." But what happens when you are Mom and Dad and Grandmother? Who is minding the store? Perhaps the "store" will be boarded up, gone away, changed, taken over by others, when *you*, the prodigal, finally decide to return.

Not all stories have happy endings. We are told that the rich young ruler in the Gospel went away sorrowing. He came close to the Truth, but not close enough. He did not find salvation because he did not put Christ first. Instead, he put his riches first.

Riches that pitch us headlong into Hell can be anything from a law degree to a successful business. Of course riches *can* literally be money, too. But riches may come packaged as academic degrees or a desire to be accepted and liked by one's secular peers. Riches can even be a desire for an easier or more dramatic Protestant or Roman Catholic-style of religious experience that takes less work than ascetic Orthodox struggle and is more superficially satisfying.

Authentic spirituality takes hard work. It takes years of struggle. It takes faithfulness. This is the lesson of the desert Fathers. We live in an undisciplined, lazy age. Our age is one where children want education to be "fun" or they refuse to learn. This mentality has produced the illiterate Sesame Street generation. Sloth and ease of life has also produced adults who want "fun," "easy" religion. They want one-stop, Protestant or Roman Catholic-style entertainments. (A friend of mine recently attended a "Circus Mass" in a large Washington D.C. Roman Catholic church, replete with clowns serving the Eucharist.) They want to be uplifted, but not to struggle. They want the gifts of the Spirit, but not the lonely fight against the unruly passions. "Touchy-feely" fellowship is a lot more fun than fasting and Holy Week vigils. Clowns and guitar-playing nuns wearing blue jeans are less demanding than strict spiritual fathers. Watching the Pope on television conducting a huge outdoor mass, and vast media circus including huge choirs and bands playing popular inspirational music is more fun than keeping a Lenten vigil.

Thankfully some lapsed Orthodox are now seeing the folly of their ways. They have tasted the bitter, empty cup of the secular culture. They have tried the sweet, fake cream puffs of modern Roman Catholic-Protestant "charismatic" religiosity. Fortunately for them, others have not been so foolish and have kept the oil lamps burning before the icons while they were out playing games in the new Babylon. Fortunately there is still

LETTER XI

an Orthodox spiritual home to which they may return. Fortunately it is not too late.

But not all the news is good. Bad habits die hard. Some of these returnees to the fold bring their desacralized, Westernized habits with them. They seek to "update" Orthodoxy, to make it more trendy and relevant. They want it "easier" and more modern. They do not want the Orthodox Church to rebuke them or to tell them not to be sexually permissive. They do not want to hear that sex outside of the sacrament of marriage is a serious sin. They do not want to hear that abortion is murder. They do not want to be told that divorce is a deadly evil. They do not want to be told not to marry a non-Orthodox. They want economy, but not obedience. They want Pascha, but never Lent. In other words, they want Disneyland, not Athos.

It must be explained to the returning Orthodox prodigals that Orthodoxy will not be Orthodox any longer if it is changed to suit their modern habits. It must be pointed out that the very things they like least about secular society—for instance, the loss of sacramental beauty and meaning—will invade Orthodoxy if they begin to try and "improve" the Church by changing it to suit their westernized tastes.

In June of 1995 I received a letter from an Australian Greek Orthodox. Let's call him Mr. T. His views seem all-too-typical of the hodge-podge of hackneyed, pluralistic, Western ideas by which many well-meaning Orthodox young adults have been infiltrated. To me this letter represents the voice of all that is most insidious and deadly to Orthodoxy's future survival in the West—the soft voice of secularism masquerading as a voice of concern for the welfare of the Orthodox Church. It is the all-too-typical mixture of half truths, ignorance, bad Orthodox teaching, and late twentieth-century "politically correct" provincialism on which so many Orthodox young adults seem to have imbibed.

> *"Our Church is greatly in need of renewal in various respects.*
> *Basing myself on my experiences in the Orthodox church and my*

LETTER XI

*studies at the Orthodox Theological College, I firmly believe that
renewal in at least the following respects is called for:*

*(1) Theological renewal. Our doctrinal heritage requires reevalua-
tion. The doctrines of the Church need to be clearly elucidated and
subjected to intensive criticism (whether it be of a positive or a negative sort). It must not be assumed that because a given doctrine
has been accepted throughout the history of the Church, it must
therefore be true. . . . Unfortunately, recent Orthodox theology (as
represented by such theologians as Lossky, Florovsky, Zizioulas, and
Yannanras) has not wholeheartedly engaged in such a reevaluation process. Rather, it has been content to expound (in an all-too-
opaque fashion) the teaching of the Byzantine Fathers. . . .*

*(2) Liturgical renewal. Here the problems are numerous. I can
only touch on a few of them. In regard to the sacraments: The introduction of adolescent baptism preceded by a period of catechesis
should be considered as a way of bringing people (who are born
into an Orthodox family) to a better appreciation of the Christian
faith (no one really believes that unbaptized babies go to hell); so
much emphasis is placed on fasting that it has become for many a
stumbling block, especially in regard to the frequent reception of
Communion. . . . Direct confession to God must be encouraged, for
confession to a priest is for many psychologically traumatic.
In regard to the Liturgy and other services . . . services need to
become more elastic and less monolithic. (Why should the Liturgy of
John Chrysotom be used almost exclusively? Why not make more
use of other liturgies, e.g., the Liturgy of James and Western-rite
liturgies such as the ancient Roman, Gallican, and Celtic liturgies?)*

*(3) Ministerial renewal. The place of the women in the ministry of
the Church requires reconsideration, especially since the Church
has clearly failed to adequately use the gifts of women. In parti-*

cular, what is required is (a) the development of the ministry of lay women by encouraging women to be more active at parish level through, e.g., preaching in the Liturgy, instructing catechumens, and serving in the sanctuary; (b) the restoration of the women's diaconate—this is long overdue; (c) serious consideration of the ordination of women to the priesthood and episcopate. . . .

(4) Monastic renewal. A much higher degree of pluralism or variation is desirable in Orthodox monasticism. There is a clear lack of monasteries which combine the life of prayer with, say, academic work (cf. the Dominicans and Jesuits) or philanthropy . . . or missionary activity. Here we have much to learn from the Catholic orders.

There are undoubtedly several other areas in which the Church is in need of renewal. Canon law is one area which quickly comes to mind—there are plenty of canons which are either inapplicable in today's world or morally reprehensible. Canons must not be seen as laws which always hold good irrespective of circumstances nor as infallible moral guides."

In the light of the letter quoted above, perhaps Orthodox prodigals need to be reminded that they are not God's gift to the Church. The Church does not need saving through modernization. In fact, the Church does not need any of us. We need Her.

We Orthodox should not tolerate a watered-down, "relevant," "modern" Orthodoxy designed to lure the prodigals back. We do not need "Orthodox" feminism, liturgical reform, or a "reevaluation" of the canons and the teaching of the Byzantine Fathers! We do not need "People's Liturgies" or "Orthodox" entertainments for young people. We cannot tolerate new "Orthodox" moral standards designed to be easy on the returnees from the new Sodom and Gomorrah. Nor do we need to "learn" from the Roman Catholics or Protestants.

LETTER XI

What we *do* need is holiness. We need monks and nuns cut from the cloth of the New Martyrs of Russia like St. Elizabeth (Grand Duchess Elizabeth). We need to keep the fasts and vigils as best we can. We need to keep our rule of prayer as best we can. We need to go to confession and receive the Eucharist frequently. We need to make pilgrimages to the holy places. We need courageous priests who will rebuke moral evil and guard the sacraments of the Church against desecration. We need bishops who will stand for the Truth. In other words, we need the mercy, salvation, and struggle that have been part and parcel of the historic Church's quest from the beginning. Above all, we need to understand that salvation only comes through struggle, and that mercy cannot operate without repentance.

As ever,
Frank

LETTER XII

Dear Fr. Aristotle,

I know, I know! It *is* "easier to diagnose the problem than prescribe a cure!" I am glad you found my last letter helpful in spite of the fact that you say that I am better at "pointing out what is wrong than at suggesting what to do about it!" I will try to do what you asked and outline a solution to the problems I mentioned *vis-a-vis* the "missing" or "lost" generation of Orthodox.

First, let me say that I am not at all sure how we can get the prodigals back. Obviously this depends on the grace of God. But perhaps there is a way for us to do our part to prevent or minimize future losses.

Most importantly, I believe that if we are to call the lost Orthodox back to the Church or prevent further attrition, the Orthodox Church must be a place full of spiritual light. In other words, plenty of secular organizations can offer Hellenic cultural events, psychological counseling, and higher critical biblical studies, but the Orthodox Church is the only place in which Christ is present in His sacramental community on earth.

We must concentrate on strengthening what is *unique* within the Orthodox Church. I do not believe that our call is to try to compete with the world. It seems to me that it is ridiculous to use secular tools like psychology or entertainment to achieve spiritual ends. This is self-defeating. The sacramental, ascetic, and spiritual must be emphasized, while the academic, social, political, and entertainment aspects of church life should be kept in perspective and subordinate to the Orthodox Church's main call.

Let me put this in another way. I believe that the first and second generations of Orthodox in America achieved a genuine miracle. Ordinary people, who were not missionaries or monks, sacrificially built churches out of the fruit of their toil and labor. They established the Orthodox presence in North America. They brought priests to America to serve their communities. This is a *magnificent achievement*. But now the question is, What must *we* do to build on this wonderful foundation?

LETTER XII

What we need to do is to actively (dare I say aggressively?) work for a spiritual revival *within* the Orthodox Church. This revival can only be achieved by introducing into the North American context the missing element of American Orthodoxy. I am speaking of monasticism and the monastic spirit of contemplation, confession, fasting, prayer, and bold evangelism.

Since America is a secular-Protestant nation, presently in a historical transition from Westernized Christianity to pure paganism, and since the whole concept of monasticism is meaningless to the desacralized Western mind (the Western churches do not believe in the possibility of divinization, and thus the ascetic struggle for perfection—to be like Christ— makes no sense), and since we Orthodox ourselves have often become secular in our mentality, therefore nothing is more important to the health of the Church than the introduction of monasticism into America.

If we have no one to imitate, how will we know how to be Christians? If monasticism is absent, how can the contemplative, ascetic, evangelistic spirit of monasticism be present in our hearts? If our only idea of a "leader" in our church is an Orthodox bureaucrat in dialogue with the apostate, how will we learn to be different than the world? How will we learn to evangelize the Protestant and secular culture with the good news of Orthodoxy? Above all, who will teach us to pray?

It is for all these reasons that I pray for the day when we have as many Orthodox monasteries, sketes, and hermitages in North America as Orthodox churches. Then the Church will truly be established here. Then it will evangelize by example. And then, and only then, will an authentic revival of Orthodox life be possible within the North American Orthodox Church. (This is not to say that we want just any kind of monastery. It must be an authentic Orthodox monastery, deeply rooted in the highly disciplined tradition of Sinai and Athos and under the guidance of a true Holy Father or Holy Mother of many years experience and from a well-established monastary.)

LETTER XII

Perhaps the establishing of monasteries will not come about all at once, although lately there have been encouraging signs that this is beginning to happen. While we wait for the Holy Spirit to bring us holy monastics, we must begin to practice the monastic rule in our own lives. For instance, we should all seek out a traditional relationship with a spiritual father and confessor. We should begin to keep, as much as possible, the calendar and the rule of prayer of the Church. Fasting can no longer be considered a joke or left "up to the individual," as if it were optional. We should teach and practice the rule of personal prayer. We should encourage pilgrimages to monastic centers of life, such as they are, here in America and to well-established, well-disciplined monasteries abroad. Above all, we must learn about the Orthodox ideal of divinization through ascetic struggle, prayer, reading of the desert Fathers, fasting, and confession and stop acting as if we can make ourselves Orthodox by merely involving ourselves in secular social activities like dances, theological studies, church politics, basketball leagues, and food festivals. Spiritual cancer is not cured with basketball! The gushing wounds of sin are not closed with donuts and coffee! Western-style theological studies are not to be confused with the prayer of the heart that saves.

I am not saying that our social activities, including theological studies, are wrong in themselves or that they should be stopped. (As the proud father of a six-foot three-inch, fourteen-year-old boy with a great fade-away shot, I am certainly not against basketball!) But we are living in delusion if we think that social activities or studies will lead people into the Orthodox way of being, let alone to God. This is why I believe it is so foolish and short-sighted to use the tricks of the world in our churches, like rock music, psychological counseling, or parties to "entice" people into the Church. The genuine article of holiness is far more attractive—even enticing—than second-rate, worldly imitations.

By beginning to put more emphasis on the spiritual discipline—that is, an essential of the Gospel of Jesus Christ—it may well mean that, for a brief time, we lose some people who now think of their church as a social club. Sadly, the number of our young adults in our churches may actually diminish for a time. However, those that remain will be the foundation of the future of Orthodoxy in our country. One person that has found the peace of God will save thousands around him. This idea is as true today as when St. Seraphim of Sarov articulated it more than a century ago.

In the end, a deep spiritual revival will attract more people (even worldly people) *and retain them* than all the tricks and bells and whistles and entertainments which, after all, the world can produce far better than we can. I know this very well. As a secular movie director and novelist, I do not long for more of what Hollywood and New York can offer. I long for what the Orthodox Church alone can offer. I did not convert to Orthodoxy because it was "trendy," but because it was true. I am not looking for psychological counseling, but for forgiveness.

It is imperative that we expose our young people (and ourselves) to authentic holiness in the persons of monks, nuns, priests, and laypeople who have practiced the ascetic way for many years. Such people make a lasting impression and give the rest of us something to aim for. This is, of course, harder to do than going to seminary, selling raffle tickets, putting on a dance, or entering into an endless and largely meaningless ecumenical "dialogue" with other ecclesiastical bureaucrats. It may *even* require that we ourselves become holy!

When it comes to teaching and education, we can no longer only teach what we are *for*. It seems to me that we also need to teach what we are *against*. For instance, we cannot simply say that God is the God of life. We also need to add that the Church is *against* abortion, infanticide, euthanasia, fetal experimentation, and the whole oppressive culture of death that surrounds us. We need to explain that it was the Fathers of the Church who stopped the practice of child sacrifice and abortion in the ancient world. We need to draw on our moral inheritance and pass it on.

Unless teaching is *specific* to the issues of our day, we are sending our children out into the world as lambs to the slaughter. There is no excuse

LETTER XII

for not teaching clearly on these matters. The declining, pagan Roman world of the early Church Fathers was much like our own. Therefore their teaching is extremely relevant to our time.

Above all, we must preach the gospel of Jesus Christ, crucified and raised from the dead. We must make a real effort to understand the culture we are in and to answer that culture with the living gospel. We must teach the Orthodox spiritual alternative to secularism, based not on one more political or utilitarian, humanistic set of psychological principles, but on *holiness of life*. In other words, we must teach our children that all of life and creation is sacred because God is the Creator and because He has sent His Son to us in order that we might be restored to our proper relationship to Him. To put it bluntly, we must seek to make ourselves and others into Christians who follow Jesus.

It is precisely the loss of the sense of the sacred that is destroying us. And it is this sacramental inheritance that the Orthodox Church must restore. It seems that this is the only true road back to recapturing and retaining our children and our children's children. It is also the only way we will come to evangelize our society.

It is the sense of the sacred that is unique and beautiful in Orthodoxy. It is this "Pearl of Great Price" that we must fight for. When we do, the lost may, by God's grace, come home.

As ever,
Frank

LETTER XIII

Dear Fr. Aristotle,

In your last letter you write about Mrs. O's idea of enrolling in a PhD program in theological studies in order that she might "deepen her understanding of Orthodox spirituality."

Let me say that I think Mrs. O. should reconsider. It seems to me that the study of theology will not bring her any closer to the heart of Orthodox Truth. This is not to say that such studies will not be very interesting, even useful. However, Orthodoxy is not something one *studies*, it is something one *does*, and by doing, one *becomes*. The problem is not with Mrs. O.'s intention to study, but with what she is hoping those studies will help her accomplish.

You are probably familiar with this anecdote. An Orthodox monk was asked by a Protestant scholar, "What is it that you Orthodox believe?" The monk answered, "You have asked the wrong question. You should rather ask, 'How is it that you Orthodox worship?'" I am sure that you understand the point. It is the same one St. Maximos and St. Evagrios make when they say something to the effect that a theologian is one who truly prays, and one who truly prays is a theologian.

The Orthodox way is very different from the Western rationalistic and scholastic method of religious inquiry. Our Orthodox history, dogma, and intellectual tradition lives in our worship. It is to be done, not only studied.

The Orthodox East never produced a Thomas Aquinas or a John Calvin (let alone a reductionist, "higher critical" method of biblical study, as if the Bible were a mere "work of literature"), because Eastern Orthodox Christians understand that one must worship with one's whole person, not just with one's mind. In other words, we pray the Scriptures—we do not merely read them. We not only care about what people believe, but about how they worship. What have you done? Who are you? What are you becoming? These are the real and only relevant questions to ask of someone in regard to the Orthodox pursuit of the Truth. The real issue is not,

LETTER XIII

What do you believe or say you believe, but rather, What are you becoming?

"As you worship, so you believe" is an old Latin saying. The Orthodox version should be, As you worship, so you become.

St. Maximos the Confessor addresses the inadequacies of an intellectual approach to the Truth. He writes:

> *"Jacob's well (cf. John 4:5-15) is Scripture. The water is the spiritual knowledge found in Scripture. The depth of the well is the mean ing, only to be attained with great difficulty, of the obscure sayings in Scripture. The bucket is learning gained from the written text of the word of God, which the Lord did not possess because He is the Logos Himself; and so He does not give believers the knowledge that comes from learning and study, but grants to those found worthy the ever-flowing waters of wisdom that spill from the fountain of spiritual grace and never run dry. For the bucket—that is to say, learning—can only grasp a very small amount of knowledge and leaves behind all that it cannot lay hold of, however it tries. But the knowledge which is received through grace, without study, contains all the wisdom that man can attain, springing forth in different ways according to his needs."*
> ("Second Century of Various Texts, 29," The Philokalia, *vol. II, pp. 193-94*)

The East mistrusts dogma and theology as a source of knowledge about God because reason is too small a "bucket" to put God and the universe into. In view of this fact, it seems to me that if Mrs. O. wishes to become truly Orthodox, she should decide what her priorities are:

(1) her ascetic journey toward Christ through fasting, confession, prayer, obedience, and participation in the communal, sacramental life in the Church.

or

LETTER XIII

(2) her theological studies.

When it comes to the second, and by far the least important, of the two categories of activity, Mrs. O. must realize that the Western vanity of the mind is just that—vanity. Life is too short (by two thousand years or so!) to begin to understand anything spiritual with our reason. According to the Fathers, to enter into the Truth we must rely not on our reason, but on our intuitive perception of Truth by our spiritual intellect.

St. Maximos the Confessor writes:

> "The law of the Old Testament through practical philosophy cleanses human nature of all defilement. The law of the New Testament, through initiation into the mysteries of contemplation, raises the intellect by means of spiritual knowledge from the sight of material things to the vision of spiritual realities."
> ("First Century of Various Texts, 67," The Philokalia, vol. II, p. 181)

To awaken our dormant spiritual intellect, we have been given the tools of obedience, fasting, prayer, ascetic struggle, and the sacraments in order to receive through grace, "all the wisdom man can attain."

Mrs. O. does not have to re-invent the wheel in order to enter into the new order, what St. Maximos calls the "law of the New Testament." Others have gone before us in showing us the way into the mysteries of contemplation. We need only do our best to imitate the Saints and the monks and to learn to pray the Jesus Prayer: "Lord Jesus Christ, Son of God, have mercy upon me, a sinner!" This is all any of us can do.

We walk not by the light of our studies and subjective personal experiences, but by the example of the entire Orthodox Church, whose Saints, Liturgy, doctrine, prayer, and monastic life we enter into. We do not need to invent new tools, but need to use the old, tried-and-true tools of faith we have inherited. Moreover, we do not need to "figure out" how to use these sacramental tools. The monks of Mt. Athos will show us the way, as will

LETTER XIII

the nuns of Ormalia and the monastics of Sinai and countless other monasteries.

What I am driving at is the fact that if Mrs. O. believes that studying theology or Byzantine, Greek, or Orthodox Church history is a way to come into the fullness of the faith, she is mistaken. Academic studies are not evil, but there is no academic route to Truth. If there were an academic route to the Truth, Orthodox seminaries would be full of holy men!

> As ever,
> Frank

LETTER XIV

Dear Fr. Aristotle,

Christ is Risen!

Thank you for your thoughtful letter. I am afraid that the casual remarks I made in the discussion period following my recent lecture at your church at this year's Lenten retreat were somewhat unclear. The point I was trying to make was that it seems that without a sense of the sacred, the secular environmental movement lacks a philosophical base for many of its best efforts and pronouncements. According to your letter I left the impression that I was "anti-environmentalist." This is not so. Let me explain.

If human beings are simply a part of nature, evolved by chance, then we cannot declare any of our actions to be unnatural, let alone immoral. We, like the rest of nature, are not free agents with souls, but merely chemically determined, evolved machines. We are just a part of nature. We happen to have evolved to rape and pillage nature as crows will pillage the nest of a house finch, given the opportunity. It makes no more sense to describe our rape of the world as "evil" than it does to criticize a queen bee for "enslaving" other bees in the hive. She and we are simply doing what comes naturally.

The great Orthodox scholar and translator of blessed memory, Philip Sherrard, makes this point far better than I could. He writes:

> "The mechanistic character of modern science is marked by a desire to dominate, to master and possess and to exploit nature, not to transform it, or to hallow it. It presumes that the earth belongs to man, not man to the earth. In this it simply reflects the self-assertion of the agent, the disinherited reason which, having completed its revolt against what surpasses it, now seeks to impose its laws over the rest of life. Man's loss of his sense of harmony and reciprocity with nature—his destruction of the nuptial bonds between them— is itself the consequence of his loss of his sense of his

status and role as the link between heaven and earth, the channel through which all commerce between them passes. . . . It is in Christ that the wall of separation between heaven and earth, the supernatural and the natural, the sacred and the profane is destroyed in the living sacrament of the divine love and presence. God's enhumanization has not only 'taken manhood into God'; it has also taken the whole created world into God, has resurrected it and transfigured it in its very depths. . . . Outside this relationship, apart from this sacrament, man has no real place in the world, or the world in him. He is but a tormented shadow of himself, and his world a forsaken wilderness, and on both he is compelled to seek ever further revenge for that crime against his own nature which he refuses to acknowledge, still more to expiate."
(The Rape of Man and Nature, *Ipswich, Suffolk, UK, 1987, pp. 40-41)*

As Sherrard points out, it is only from the religious perspective that the human race is specifically endowed with moral responsibility. Only if we were created for a high moral purpose does the call to repent in any area of human activity, including our misuse of nature, make sense.

To the extent that the members of the modern environmental movement, or members of any other secularized "moral crusade" for that matter, are atheistic or secular in their philosophy, they have no rational basis on which to pronounce any ecological or other action as right or wrong. The secular environmental movement is left with nothing more than purely utilitarian reasons for its ethics since it has no belief in the otherness or spiritual uniqueness of man.

To the humanist, the atheist, or the agnostic, we are just part of nature. This leaves us with no ultimate reason as to why it is "right" to save nature or "wrong" to despoil it. For instance, secular environmentalists may argue that we should save the rain forests because of the medicinal value of the many plants hidden in its gloomy depths. But if some plants turn out to have no medicinal or other specific, utilitarian value, the secularist has no

LETTER XIV

basis to plead for them to be spared destruction other than subjective sentiment. And even if certain plants are specifically useful to mankind, the secular environmentalist has not made a case as to why the survival of the human species is important.

Who is to say that the survival of any species, including ours, is intrinsically important in a mechanistic, chemically determined, morally silent universe? Without a sense of created and ultimate spiritual purpose, who cares about the fate of the earth? After all, would we lament the extinction of the polio virus? We do not regret the vast silences of outer space. Why should we care about the Bengal tiger or the human race?

It is all very well to say we should be stewards of the earth, but stewards are appointed, not self-made. Anyway, who is to determine what it means to be a steward? Whom should we imitate? Perhaps we should imitate a colony of soldier ants and "obey our instincts" and destroy and consume all before us. Perhaps the desertification of the whole planet is our true chemically determined, biological call.

It must be pointed out that just as the secular, academic, and artistic communities must borrow a vocabulary of spiritual meaning (i.e., words such as *beauty, love, right,* and *wrong*) from a religious and specifically Christian dogma, so too the modern environmental movement is somewhat naive, at best, and disingenuous, at worst.

Modern environmentalists borrow the language of free will, choice, and created moral purpose (such as stewardship of the earth or committing sins against the environment) when it is convenient to do so. They borrow this language of morality and purpose from our Christian religious system while denying the ultimate truth of that system. Ironically, some environmentalists even attack Christianity and blame it for the rape of the planet. Evidently they have never been to Mt. Athos to see how the monks care for the earth they have been given!

As ever,
Frank

LETTER XV

Dear Fr. Aristotle,

Thank you for your comments on the new translation of the Holy Week service book. I also take note of your observations regarding the whole issue of "gender inclusive" language and the use of vernacularized, or "ordinary," English in the services of the Orthodox Church.

Coincidentally, in the same post in which I received your letter, another friend of mine, a woman who is a recent convert to Orthodoxy from Roman Catholicism, wrote to me about the same issues. She writes that her priest has suddenly taken to vernacularizing the Liturgy. For instance, she says that he is dropping the more formal English usage of words such as *Thee* and *Thou* in favor of *you*. My friend says that her priest has also begun to correct the liturgical language of the Church by changing words such as *mankind* to *humankind* or *people* in accordance with the current politically correct "gender inclusive" fashions of American academia and the popular press. She writes, "He makes the Liturgy sound everyday, as if he's a TV broadcaster reading the news. . . . He seems to think this is a great idea. But it leaves me cold. I feel as if I'm reading one of those awful 'dumbed down' new textbooks where some goofy, second-rate writer is paraphrasing Shakespeare for children—you know, '*Hamlet*, as retold by Joe Blow'."

My friend writes that during Holy Week this year, her priest was using the same new translation of the Holy Week services that you wrote to me about. She said that gender inclusive language is employed in this translation and that the late Fr. Leonidas Contos of blessed memory, the translator, has edited the text and cut various traditional passages, particularly the Holy Thursday tones and prayers, that he apparently believed are offensive to Jews. My friend (she teaches anthropology at a university in Boston) says that such arbitrary antitraditional innovations fill her with dismay. She writes, "I had expected better of the Orthodox. . . . Perhaps I was naïve. This all makes me so tired. . . . I have seen this so-called liturgical reform before in my former life as a Roman Catholic. . . . Please, *please* tell me this is just an aberration and not the wave of the future. . . . Don't these

LETTER XV

people know where all this will lead?" Her comments and yours seem to be more or less identical regarding this matter.

My friend's letter and yours raise a number of very important concerns. Issues related to worship, liturgy, and translation cut to the very heart of the Orthodox faith. Our Tradition lives primarily in our liturgical prayers and tones. Whoever controls the liturgical language of the Church controls Orthodoxy. It seems to me that these questions should be discussed openly and given careful thought by *all* Orthodox, and that translations should not be left to the tender mercies of the "experts." Nor should liturgical reform be disguised as translation.

After I received your letter, I purchased a copy of the new Holy Week translation you wrote to me about. In the introduction, Fr. Contos admits to making changes in the text. He claims that his editorial innovations reflect the fact that we live in more enlightened times. He writes:

> *"The [original Greek] texts contain many references to the Jewish people. For us . . . [the original Greek tones and prayers] have the ring of prejudice. Wherever possible, and permissible within the context, such anti-Semitic elements have been tempered by concern for the worshiper's sensitivity, and the more enlightened attitude that prevails today."*

I find this statement very curious. It seems to provide no valid reason to delete passages from the ancient Holy Week prayers and services beyond one person's, or one committee's, arbitrary and highly disputable judgment that the Orthodox Church's worship is "anti-Semitic."

From a purely historical point of view, I scarcely know what to say of the idea that the blood-drenched, supremely decadent twentieth century is of all times enlightened, or, that in the context of the debauch of modern America, more "enlightened attitudes prevail today." I am also perplexed by the unsupported, almost casual observation that the Orthodox Church's Holy Week worship is anti-Semitic. The fact that an Orthodox priest would write such a thing about the supreme treasures of his Church is quite astounding. One wonders how any priest could expect any other priest to place a text containing this inflammatory and anti-Orthodox statement on the altar of an Orthodox Church.

The late Fr. Contos' remarks are particularly bewildering to me because, as an acquaintance of his, I had a high regard for him and the many years of outstanding service he gave to the Orthodox Church. Perhaps in this instance we are seeing the sort of "blind spot" that we all have in one area or another. It is only unfortunate that this particular blind spot seems to have been manifested in something as important as the integrity of the texts of the Holy Week services. Statements such as those made by Fr. Contos demand some sort of an answer since they are in such a public and important context.

Since none of us operate in a vacuum, we should take note of the context in which Fr. Contos and other translators have been working. The modern academic context is one in which the tyranny of so-called political correctness is pervasive. This is especially true when it comes to the use of the English language.

In recent years, particularly since the 1960s, a concerted effort has been made to use the English language as an ideological weapon. In other words, an effort has been made to alter the language in order to make it a vehicle through which to push a political agenda. This linguistic weapon has been fashioned by people holding to an antitraditional philosophy that has a definitely secular and antireligious flavor. In fact, the first academic ideologues who began to change the English language and to bend it to their purposes were Marxists. They and other ideologues have understood all too well the adage, "As a man thinketh, so is he."

Today the Marxist manipulation of the English language has been imitated by many ideologically motivated groups, most notably the feminists. As a result, whole departments have been created in our universities to push the feminist worldview onto the rest of the culture by subtle—and not so subtle—changes in the English language itself. The whole use of so-called gender neutral language (for instance, in changing words such as *mankind* to *humankind* or *people*) has been but a small part of a much larger campaign to radically alter the way we speak and think. While some of the details of this campaign may seem trivial or minor, the total effect has been dramatic and far-reaching.

From the feminist point of view, the campaign to revise the English language makes good sense. The way we think about things is indeed shaped in part by the words we use to describe the world around us. Through linguistic "reform," the feminist agenda has subtly infiltrated the general culture. The feminists have successfully coerced, bullied, and convinced many writers in the popular media, and the authors of textbooks as well, to adopt their so-called gender neutral or gender inclusive forms of language. Not only have the feminists accomplished a present-day linguistic revolution, they have also retroactively commandeered the past. Feminist literary studies have rewritten the history of literature into a history of gender struggle and patriarchal "tyranny."

When we consider the use of modern feminist forms of speech in the context of Orthodox worship, we have to frankly acknowledge that the use of such "gender neutral" language is not neutral at all. Nor is it a mere "detail." Rather it represents the politicizing of the Liturgy. In fact, the mere adoption of such terminology has many unseen ramifications, because our English language itself is now caught up in what have been called the "culture wars" of our day. These culture wars pit the so-called Knowledge Class against those men and women who hold to a more traditional view of life. This Knowledge Class—members of the leftist, feminist, and Marxist student movement of the 1960s—has now become "the establishment" and have imported their ideologies into the arts, media, and universities. They are sometimes referred to as "the tenured Left." Their efforts have been felt in theological circles, including Orthodox circles as well as on secular campuses.

The Knowledge Class has been very specific and frank in its aims. One of them is to rewrite the English language to serve as a propaganda tool to

LETTER XV

use in an effort to root out the last vestiges of perceived social inequities like "sexism," "homophobia," and all other threats, real or imagined, to total social egalitarianism. This effort has even been codified in a number of books. For instance, *Guidelines for Bias-Free Writing* by Marilyn Schwartz and the Task Force on Bias-Free Language of the Associates of American University Presses (Indiana, 1995) is one such codification. In this "handbook," a very frank attempt is made to enforce the feminist, homosexual, and leftist rewriting of the English language.

The Task Force on Bias-Free Language is quite open in its aims. It seeks to set a standard to which all academic writers will be forced to adhere. If they do not follow the "guidelines," the authors are quite clear as to what the result will be. Deviation from the norm will be punished. Recalcitrant authors will not be published, at least not by the academic presses in North America.

In *Guidelines* the Task Force exhibits a total disregard for the truth that goes so far as to urge blatant dishonesty upon translators. It says translators should make up their own minds "about whether gender-biased characteristics of the original warrant replication in English."

Lest anyone mistake the coercive intent involved in such "suggestions," the powerful Association of American University Presses (AAUP) makes its position on what it will or will not publish very clear. The position statement adopted by the AAUP board of directors in November of 1992 reads:

> *"Books that are on the cutting edge of scholarship should also be at the forefront in recognizing how language encodes prejudice. They should be agents for change and the redress of past mistakes."*

In their handbook the AAUP makes it abundantly clear that what they mean by language that "encodes prejudice" includes anything that deviates from the most radically defined feminist and leftist use of language. Indeed, traditional Christian expression is specifically singled out as unacceptable. Traditional or hierarchical forms of Christian expression are especially frowned upon. Clearly God, at least traditional notions of God, are out. The God of the Bible is too notorious for His "bias" in favor of certain minorities, for the gross "inequities" of His Creation, and for His politically incorrect "sin" of revealing Himself as a Man in the Incarnation.

In a recent article in *Commentary*, Wendy Shalit, a young writer studying at Williams College, wrote an illuminating piece that vividly captures the flavor of the present-day life on American campuses as it has been shaped by the same forces that have worked so hard to coerce linguistic obedience to feminist ideology.

The portion quoted below perfectly describes the near-fascist conformity of present-day campus life due to the absolutist nature of so-called political correctness.

> *"I am sometimes puzzled by all the talk in universities these days about the loss of the canon. My own liberal arts college, at any rate, most certainly has not lost its. To be sure, our canon is not comprised of those much-maligned Great Books. Instead there is our required course on 'Peoples and Cultures'; there is the astonishing array of sensitivity and 'safe sex' sessions which freshmen are forced to attend; and there are the harassment codes to which we must strictly adhere. These immediately introduce us, if not to the best that has been thought and said, then at least to the worst canonical biases of our time.*

> *The prerequisite for appreciating the Old Canon was simply a willingness, in the eloquent formulation of W.E.B. Du Bois, to engage ideas 'above the Veil.' ('Across the color line I move arm and arm with Balzac. . . . So, wed with Truth, I dwell above the Veil.') The prerequisites for entry into the New Canon are more daunting, involving, among other things, a talent for overlooking contradictions: one must not be racist, sexist, or ethnocentric unless one happens to be black or a woman; one must be positively sympathetic to diversity of gender, race, and sexual orientation but not to diver-*

sity of ideas; One must never admit a devotion to truth except to the truth embodied in the harassment code; one must deride the 'notion' of historical fact but never question the facts of those who tell their own 'survivor stories'; one must cleanse oneself of fidelity to the fixed meaning of texts, except to the texts of the postmodernists. Equipped with such understanding, the would-be adept of the New Canon may dive right in.

But what is left to dive into? If studying the Old Canon required only an ability to transcend the cultural Veil, the parameters of study—man and his nature—were breathtakingly limitless. The opposite is true of the New Canon, where the prerequisites are seemingly limitless while the object of study—oneself, one's own origins—is of a quite narrow scope. If an Old Canon student could echo the Roman playwright Terence, 'I am a man: nothing human is alien to me,' the student entrapped in the New Canon seems to be forever chanting the dirge, 'I am my gender, race, and sexual orientation: Everything *human is alien to me, except for my gender, race, and sexual orientation. . .'*

The New Canon makes its presence felt immediately, in freshman orientation. At my college, this mandatory ritual consists of, among other things, a 'Feel-What-It-Is-Like-To-Be-Gay' meeting. Our Bisexual, Gay, and Lesbian Union (BGLU) representatives tour the freshman dorms and require each student to declare, 'Hello, my name is [freshman inserts his/her name here] and I'm gay!'

Next comes National Community Building Workshop (NCBW), a day-long program in which each freshman is required to join a group and compose a list of insults he or she does not want to be called, as in 'I'm a woman—don't call me a chick!' or 'I'm Hispanic—don't call me a Spic!' At my NCBW I humbly offered 'conservative' as my preferred group, and for my insult, 'Don't call me a free-market apologist!' There was considerable uncertainty about whether this counted. . . .

LETTER XV

Later that week, at a session on 'Race, Gender, Identity, and Community,' all the students in my freshman class were herded into a darkened auditorium. There we were asked to keep our eyes closed while various slurs were hurled at us from all directions. This marked the conclusion of 'diversity sensitivity,' and rounded out our freshman orientation.

Having been thus introduced to the New Canon, perhaps I should not have been surprised when, this past year, our administration waived the rule against defacing campus property just in time for the Bisexual, Gay, and Lesbian Union to chalk our buildings and sidewalks with obscenities, the better to celebrate National Coming-Out Week. Nor should I have been surprised that in addition to National Coming-Out Week we had Women's Pride Week, and Students of Mixed Heritage Week, and Queer Pride Week, and Bisexual Visibility Week, Latino/Latina Awareness Week, and Eating Disorders Awareness Week. After all, maintaining the proper climate of moral correctness demands constant reinforcement, and if anyone should object, the Dean's Office is ready to respond swiftly with an all-campus mailing."
(Shalit, Wendy, "A Ladies' Room of One's Own," in Commentary, *August 1995)*

It is in the context of the very illiberal "liberalism" described above that the Orthodox academic and translator of today operates. He or she may lead a comparatively sheltered life within the Orthodox community, but nevertheless is naturally not unaffected by the climate of the larger academic community. It is in this modern context that new translations of Orthodox sacred texts must be evaluated. They must not simply be evaluated on the surface, but also for what hidden baggage of the new "liberal" canon or assumptions they carry.

In the volatile world of feminist and leftist academic coercion, Orthodox translators should be clear in their intent and honest about their aims. And

LETTER XV

we Orthodox laity should also be clear as to what we require of our translators. Our translators should be required to show us exactly what is Orthodox about the new language they use in their translations. The Orthodox faithful should not accept or tolerate a *fait accompli* when it comes to liturgical translations. Nor should we tolerate the notion that somehow the issue of language has already been decided someplace by someone (perhaps by the Task Force of the Association of American University Presses!) and that all further discussion is precluded. Nor should we buy into the notion that the "experts" teaching in our seminaries have some special insight into the spiritual inheritance of the Church.

Before Orthodox translators begin to import the ideology of the 1960s "New Left" and the terminology of the Marxist-Feminist linguistic crusade into the Holy Texts of the Church, they must show why this is a good thing. The fact that "everyone else is doing it," or "we need to keep up with the times," is not an Orthodox argument at all.

However, it is exactly this kind of *fait accompli* that seems to prevail in many current efforts of translation and liturgical reform, both in Orthodox and non-Orthodox religious circles. The idea seems to be that if our academic elites lead, we must follow. This, however, is a very un-Orthodox idea.

Orthodoxy is a "bottom-up" religion. The least monk or layman has not only the right but the duty to question the leadership of the Church if it seems to be departing from Holy Tradition. And in this light, it seems that an open, even brutally frank, discussion of the whole idea of liturgical reform and new translation is in order. The stakes are very high indeed.

I am certainly no linguist, let alone a liturgical expert. Please allow me, therefore, to direct your attention to the opinions of one of the most respected Orthodox scholars and modern translators of Greek texts into English. I am referring to the late Professor Philip Sherrard, of blessed memory, who, as you know, authored many books on Greek literary and historical themes and won international acclaim for his translation work on such sacred texts as *The Philokalia* (Faber and Faber, London, 1979), and

LETTER XV

for his translations of such modern Greek poets as Cavafy, Sikelianos, Seferis, and Elytis. (Professor Sherrard converted to Orthodoxy in 1953. He taught Greek and Orthodox Church history at the Universities of Oxford and London. He lived for many years in Katounia, Greece, until his death in the spring of 1995.)

As an eminent scholar of Greek, Greek history, and Orthodoxy, a renowned translator, and most importantly, by all accounts, a holy and pious Orthodox Christian, Professor Sherrard's views on Orthodox Holy Tradition, our contemporary culture, and the Church are highly relevant to questions of how the Church should respond to innovative "translations," particularly as they relate to our sacred texts and how these translations might effect the quality of our worship.

In his seminal study, *The Greek East and the Latin West* (Oxford University Press, 1959), Professor Sherrard argues that one of the fundamental differences between the East and West is that in the Orthodox Church we place great store not only in Holy Mystery but in intuitive spiritual revelation through the process of mystical initiation. By contrast, he writes, the Western churches, Roman and Protestant, place more faith in human reason. It seems that Professor Sherrard is saying that if we begin to act as if the purpose of the Liturgy and Orthodox worship is *educational* or *political* rather than *sacramental*, we will undermine the very essence of Orthodoxy.

Professor Sherrard writes:

> *"Where Christianity is concerned, there is an intimate connection between doctrine and method: the Truth of the doctrine, that which doctrinal formulations not only 'reveal' but also 'conceal', is, in its essential and universal nature, something that can be known only by one who is 'initiated' into it through following the discipline of the Christian Way itself. It is not something which man can arrive at through the unaided processes of human thought. It transcends the reason, It transcends logic. Rational and logical demonstrations*

are only 'true,' and this in a relative sense, provided that they begin in, and develop from, an a priori *realization of what is in itself supra-rational and supra-logical. If they do not begin in, and develop from, such a realization, but merely in and from some arbitrary fiat of the human mind, what they represent is no more than a blind and unreal operation, lacking all objective validity. Logic is but the science of mental coordination and of arriving at rational conclusions from a given starting-point. If the starting-point is a supra-logical 'visionary' knowledge of the Truth attained through initiation, then logic has a positive content in the way we have indicated. But if man merely 'thinks' of the Truth with his mind, then all his logic is useless to him because he starts with an initial fallacy, the fallacy that the Truth can be attained by the unaided processes of human thought.*

This fallacy is that I have described as the philosophical mentality. The philosophical mentality assumes that logic and the reason are in themselves capable of arriving at the Truth." (The Greek East and Latin West, *p. 56)*

Professor Sherrard argues that in Orthodox worship we Orthodox should understand the sacramental value of the *doing* of worship rather than merely seeing worship as a verbal learning experience. If Professor Sherrard is correct, and the ultimate value of worship is in our participation in mystical sacramental acts, then why would an Orthodox priest or translator seek to make the purely verbal aspects of worship more politically correct, "acceptable," "sensitive," or "understandable" by vernacularizing the text or updating it? Surely such psychologically, politically, or sociologically motivated innovation will almost always be at the expense of the Orthodox sense of the timeless and sacred nature of the Truth? Surely efforts to change the traditional content of the Greek texts, when they are put into English, show that the translator has adopted the Western philosophical mentality that pervades such organizations as the Association of

LETTER XV

American University Presses (not to mention the World and National Council of Churches) and that he is willing to sacrifice Orthodox purity and the stability of the Orthodox community on the altar of Western learning and political fashion?

All of this brings up a question: If worship is *worship*, not mere abstract teaching, entertainment, or education, then why cannot it exist in its own right, apart from the common fashions, political sensitivities, or vulgarities of the moment? Why does worship have to keep up with the times as if it were a commercial product or a political candidate seeking votes in a pluralistic society?

As Professor Sherrard writes:

> *"To assume, as modern historians often do, that what [lies behind issues of church history, worship, and doctrine] which involved some of the greatest minds of Christendom, and even, indeed, saints, [are] but factors of a political, economic, or cultural nature, reveals, to say the least, an astonishing impudence, of a kind only possible in an age in which the understanding of anything that surpasses the material level has practically ceased to exist."*
> (The Greek East and Latin West, p. 50)

The basic fallacy of Western, and hence North American, culture is that we have adopted precisely the materialistic worldview Sherrard denounces. The result is that we are in love with change for its own sake, since we believe in evolutionary "progress" rather than changeless Truth. Because of this, nothing is held to be sacred, let alone changeless. Everything becomes a political tool for change, including language and even translation work.

It is in the context of our empty love affair with all things "new" and "improved" that language has become a politicized, rationalistic, utilitarian tool. It has been reduced to the lowest common denominator, along with

LETTER XV

just about every other aspect of American culture. And like so much of our culture (literature and art), language too has been grossly politicized by every political group from Marxists and feminists to homosexuals. As we have seen, this politicizing has now been codified in our universities. But from the Orthodox point of view, language is a creation of God. In fact, the Fathers teach that human communication is rooted in the communication of the three Persons of the Trinity.

God has revealed Himself to us through language (revelation), as well as through the rest of creation and the Incarnation. Like all of creation, language is infused with the sacred. God has created language as the instrument whereby we can communicate Truth in our priestly duty of discerning the sacred in all creation and in offering it back to Him. In this regard it seems that it is not coincidental that Christ is described as "the Word"— the Word that became flesh, thereby (among other things) raising the intrinsic worth of language to a new height.

Christ spoke, read, argued, and prayed out loud. Language was thus reconsecrated by Christ. We know that Christ Himself used language carefully. Indeed, He chose to give extraordinary literary and poetic shape to His words. Rather than vernacularizing or reducing His message to the most understandable or lowest common denominator, He chose to speak in complex parables. In fact, Christ's disciples often complained that they could not understand what Christ said. As for the common people, much of what Christ taught was hidden from them. "Therefore speak I to them in parables; because they seeing see not; and hearing they hear not, neither do they understand" (Matthew 13:13). Clearly more was at work in Christ's ministry on earth than simplistic verbal communication.

It seems that, from the Orthodox point of view, language is not merely a tool to be used or abused in order to convey symbolic knowledge, let alone to make us "feel good about ourselves" or to help us "progress." Rather, language is something important in itself. Language has intrinsic value and, as such, the way something is said is often as important as what is being said. Truly form does follow function. (Indeed, the feminists understand this principle all too well.) And in the case of the language of worship, its form should be the highest form of communication of all.

As ever,
Frank

LETTER XVI

Dear Fr. Arisitotle,

The desert monks of St. Michael's Skete in New Mexico (a desert out-post of the Monastery of the Glorious Ascension in Georgia, O.C.A.) publish an important and illuminating journal. This quarterly review, *Doxa*, recently dedicated an entire issue to the proper use of liturgical language. The excerpt I quote below constitutes one of the best statements about the proper use of English in Orthodox worship that I have ever read:

> *"Our concern in fact is not one of mere conservatism or some sort of mindless traditionalism, nor is it a question of competition between 'Old English' and 'Modern English.' The challenge of liturgical language is not an old versus new issue at all:* **It is a question of quality**. . . . *Liturgical language, the sacramental word, is nothing less than verbal iconography. A verbal icon, that is to say, a liturgical text, like any other icon, must be holy—it must be set apart by respect-inspiring boundaries. The many and varied veils and covers used in Orthodox worship, from the iconostasis and vestments to the chalice veil and the curtains on the Royal Doors, at one and the same time both reveal ('re-veil') and conceal, thereby eliciting our reverence. The verbal icon must also be 'veiled'—it should be decently and appropriately clothed in excellent poetic and artistic language. Of course this language must be understandable. That is not at issue. But the language of liturgy should also appeal to the senses, speak to the heart, and engage the mind of the worshiper. And like any other icon, the liturgical text must be* kalos, *a work of beauty, as well as an accurate translation faithfully representing its original. Anything less is not 'adequate' (Greek,* prepet), *that is, suitable, appropriate, to the Orthodox Faith.*

> *Throughout the Orthodox jurisdictions in this country people are innocently parroting a mistaken notion about liturgical language which has invaded the Church from non-Orthodox sources. We are speaking of the idea that the quality of liturgical language is of no consequence—the only issue is that people should be able to under*

stand, without the least bit of effort, what is being said in the Liturgy. . . .

The idea that the quality of liturgical language counts for little reflects, among other things, current American pandering to the lowest common denominator, a perversion of the democratic ideal which has made our public education system among the worst on earth. . . .

It should not go without notice that the greatest promoters of pedestrian translations among the heterodox have been those who abhor the traditional dogmas of Christianity, who believe doctrines are merely personal opinions, and whose view of Christ is far from that of the Holy Tradition. Among their number we also find the denominational leaders, Protestant and Roman Catholic alike, most influenced by, and who most propagate, a secular humanist interpretation of Christianity. The latter clearly have a socio-political agenda in moving radically away from traditional language. They know this helps wean people off 'undesirable' traditional values— i.e. values that don't square with the current values of 'liberal' thinking. . . .

A Liturgical Movement [in Protestant, Anglican and Roman Catholic Churches] which began some thirty-five years ago with a clarion call to the corporate participation of the People of God in the glory of liturgical worship and the beauty of holiness, quickly degenerated into a celebration of the banal. The liturgical use of common everyday English was supposed to create across the board renewal, but the history of those denominations where the change was instituted has been far from encouraging—attendance at services of worship and financial support, for instance, have dropped radically, as much as one third or more in some churches. On the other hand, the fastest growing denominational Christian bodies are conservative groups which continue to use the 'King

LETTER XVI

James Bible'. In addition, the fact that the Book of Mormon is written in 'King James English' doesn't seem to be impeding Mormon missionary success one bit. In all these cases, there is without any doubt a significant degree of correspondence between the type of language used in Scripture and worship, and the temporal health of the institution. . . . Not far below the surface of the notion that the quality of liturgical language is of no great significance lurk two major theological viruses in company with a philosophical malady. Operating in clandestine synergy these three, injected into the question of liturgical translations, deliver a damaging dosage of error with destructive results.

The philosophical malady is 'Intellectual Darwinism,' the shallow belief that only the latest trends and the newest ideas or practices are 'relevant'. Of the two theological viruses, one is the minimalism and reductionism which has afflicted theology in the West for centuries, which we have called 'merely-ism'. It would have us believe that since language is merely a tool for communicating facts, street English is just fine in church. The other serious theological error is a grave misunderstanding of the Incarnation, which dates back to the early Western Middle Ages, which we have named 'upside-down' or 'inverse' Incarnationism. It is upside-down because it turns the doctrine of the Incarnation on its head.

Inverse Incarnationalism tends to view the Incarnation as the reduction of the Godhead to flesh, rather than as the assumption, and consequent elevation, of human nature by a Divine Person. It sees the Incarnation as the lowering of God to the human level, rather than as the exaltation of human nature into sublime union with God. . . . The Orthodox doctrine of the Incarnation views the entrance of Christ into this world but as the first movement in the Transfiguration of the Cosmos. The fact that the eternal King of Glory, even the Lord of Hosts, 'emptied Himself' (what the Scriptures call 'kenosis') to be born in a stable and laid in a manger, is not a sign that church buildings and all that pertains to Christian worship ideally should be of manger quality. The kenosis of Christ means rather that the Lord Himself descended to be born in a lowly cattle shed precisely that He might initiate, from the bottom up as it were, the Deification of Man and the Metamorphosis of the whole Creation.

Based squarely on the Orthodox Doctrine of the Incarnation, the Orthodox Sacramental Tradition calls us to offer to God in church the very best we have—good bread and wine, quality olive oil, gracious architecture, well-executed art work, the most suitable music, the best language, and so on and so forth. The question of liturgical translations for the Orthodox Church is therefore nothing less than a major issue relating directly to sacramental theology. If that fact is not stressed in traditional Orthodox writings, it is surely because earlier Orthodox liturgical translators and writers took it as a given so obvious to one and all that it didn't need to be pointed out.

The belief that the Koiné Greek and the Slavonic of the Scriptures and the Liturgy are 'just plain old street languages' is an unhistorical fantasy conjured up to serve inverse-Incarnational thinking imported into some Orthodox circles. Yes, Koiné Greek was the Common Greek of the ancient world, the business and street language of the Roman Empire. But the language of the Scriptures is Koiné filtered and refined, first century Greek at its very best. That is particularly clear in the Gospel of John. There, even though the grammar and syntax are very much simpler than we find in classical Greek, the Gospel text is nevertheless artistically complex, intricately organized, and replete with double and triple meanings, subtle irony, and myriad mystical allusions connecting the mission of the Lord to Old Testament themes. And all of this is couched in a sublimely poetic and flowing literary style. That is hardly the everyday language of commerce and the streets!

LETTER XVI

As for Church Slavonic, to create it, two Greek brothers, Saints Cyril and Methodios, literally spent years in monastic seclusion refining the language of the Slavs who lived in the vicinity of their native Thessalonica, which language the brothers had spoken fluently from childhood. The result was a liturgical tongue adequate to Orthodox worship and understandable to all Slavs who knew the basics of the Christian Faith. The Greek Orthodox brothers cared enough for another ethnos, namely the Slavs, to respect their need for a sophisticated literary language. Their Slavic barbarian beneficiaries in their turn were no fools. For they knew full well that the possession of such a splendid literary tongue would number them among the civilized tribes of the Byzantine Commonwealth, and they gratefully accepted the gift. . . .

Contrary to [some] 'conventional wisdom,' it is not merely time and use in church which transformed Koiné Greek, Church Slavonic and Tudor English into revered tongues. The passage of time and centuries of use definitely do enhance respect for a liturgical language—it is very human, in the best sense of that word, to regard as hallowed time-honored and noble works of art. But the actual transformation of liturgical texts from mundane to holy was wrought on the very day the Greek, Slavic, or Tudor English authors or translators of those texts, endowed by God with outstanding verbal skills, performed their sacred task. To emulate the standard set by those gifted crafters of liturgical language is the challenge facing today's Orthodox translators, as well as composers of new liturgical material."
(Brother Isaac, Doxa: A Quarterly Review Serving the Orthodox Church, *Cañones, New Mexico, 1994)*

In the light of the remarkable statement quoted above, the following questions deserve some consideration by all Orthodox laymen, monks, priests, and bishops.

LETTER XVI

1. What are the appropriate limits that a priest or chanter should observe in ad-libbing changes in the wording of the Orthodox liturgies and prayers?

2. At what point does ad-libbing and/or use of vernacularization or gender inclusive language subtly change the meaning of sacred texts? When does a priest's liturgical "editing" become scandalous, offensive, distracting, or even heretical? (For instance, by de-emphasizing the Fatherhood of God, the incarnational Manhood of Christ, the femininity of the Theotokos, or the apophatic otherness and mystery of worship?)

3. At what point do feminized, inclusive language "translations" introduce a new neo-pagan gnosticism into the Orthodox Church by virtue of association with the political feminist agenda? (The feminist movement has encouraged the resurgence of earth worship, pagan goddess worship, child sacrifice in abortion, and lesbian "liberation." Feminist theologians have even resurrected the Gnostic gospels which they now use instead of, or with, the canonical Scriptures.)

4. Is the lowest common linguistic denominator in worship always best? Is there no place for a formal, sacred, or high iconic and beautifully poetic language that separates the formal act of worship from mundane daily life?

5. What purpose is served by introducing new English language translations of our Orthodox services into the Church at this time?

6. Are nontraditional versions of the Liturgy used by Greek-speaking Greek Orthodox in Greek-speaking churches in America? Is liturgical reform masquerading as new translations allowed in churches using Church Slavonic or Arabic? Is this kind of editorial innovation something reserved only for the unfortunate English-speaking Orthodox?

7. Do the priests, bishops, and translators of the Greek and Russian Orthodox Churches here in North America have sufficient sensitivity toward the rich poetic, literary, and cultural nuances of the English lan-

guage? Do they love the English language? Do they understand that for English speakers it is the only liturgical language we have? Do they know that, to the Western ear, using words like *you* for God instead of *Thee* and *Thou* implies a subtle lack of respect, not to mention utter linguistic taste-lessness and lack of poetry?

8. Are the revisionist fashions of late twentieth-century America going to become normative in the historic Church?

9. Shall we now edit our Church's history to suit the tastes of our modern anti-Christian and multicultural Knowledge Class?

10. Is the job of a translator of Orthodox material to please his interfaith colleagues at the expense of our Holy Tradition?

11. Why would an Orthodox priest wish to become an accessory to the "dumbing down" of America?

12. When Saints Cyril and Methodios evangelized the Slavs, they brought them the light of Greco-Byzantine-Orthodox culture; they did not contribute to the delinquency of Slavic pagan backwardness. In fact, they gave the Slavs the gift of high linguistic expression. Will the Orthodox Church play this civilizing role in our own pagan nation?

13. When Vladimir sent his emissaries to Constantinople, they reported that they had found the place where God dwelt with men. They said, "We knew not whether we were in heaven or on earth." Was this because the worship they observed in the Great Church of Holy Wisdom was common, everyday, mundane, inclusive, vernacularized, sensitive to diversity, politically correct, and Western? Was it because the Byzantines believed in the moral equivalency of all cultures and religions?

14. Will American Orthodox priests pass on the light they have been entrusted with by their forefathers?

LETTER XVI

Clearly language, especially the language of worship, must be treated with the same spiritual reverence with which all of creation should be treated by those who try to see reality as it is—in other words, try to see things as God sees them.

We should refuse to deform sacramental language through the secular lens of reductionist utilitarianism, just as we refuse to deform the sacraments. In my opinion, Orthodox translators who consciously or unconsciously bend to the will of our academic "liberal" elite are not worthy to be given the great responsibility of translating the sacred texts of the Orthodox Church.

As ever,
Frank

LETTER XVII

Dear Fr. Aristotle,

The Fathers teach us that the spiritual intellect (including the spiritual intellect of a priest, no doubt) is not merely a rational or scientific instrument. Rather, the intellect is supposed to be part of the whole transcendent person.

St. Maximos the Confessor writes:

> *"When a man's intellect is constantly with God, his desire grows beyond all measure into an intense longing for God. . . . For by continual participation in the divine radiance his intellect becomes totally filled with light . . . filling it with an incomprehensible and intense longing for Him and with unceasing love, thus drawing it entirely away from worldly things to the divine."*
> *("Second Century On Love,"* The Philokalia, *vol. II, p. 73)*

Surely Orthodox priests should not take it upon themselves to update, vernacularize, or simplify the Liturgy and other services of the Church. And surely translations of the holy texts should be done in the spirit of St. Maximos, in a way that draws them "entirely away from worldly things to the divine."

Perhaps in view of how important language is to worship, it is not coincidental that all cultures and all religions have developed and guarded a special holy language or high language reserved for worship. As we have seen in the wonderful piece I sent you from *Doxa* in my last letter, this high or holy tongue may well be understood by the common man, but *it* is not common.

I believe that we should consider the question of vernacularization (or "dumbing down") and liturgical innovation within the Orthodox community in the light of the experiences of other Christian bodies.

LETTER XVII

An important article from Peter L. Berger, the well-known Lutheran scholar, author, and professor of sociology at Boston University is instructive in regard to the Orthodox. In a brilliant article published in *First Things* (April 1995) titled "The Vernacularist Illusion," he writes:

> *"In recent decades, both among Roman Catholics and Protestants, there has been much talk about liturgical reform and a great amount of activity resulting from this talk. Some people have even described these developments as a liturgical revolution.*
>
> *There have been different theological and pastoral rationales given for the changes in worship, and, of course, some changes have been more radical than others. But there is one central assumption that underlies most of the changes—namely, that the traditional, pre-reform modes of worship were too remote from the lives of ordinary people and that the language of worship had become incomprehensible. Much of the liturgical reform of recent decades was consequently a great turn toward the vernacular. To be sure, there have been other motives, notably those that have animated the promoters of so-called 'inclusive language,' which is a political project designed to change the content rather than the comprehensibility of liturgical language. In a wider sense, however, this project too is related to the vernacular urge, for that political project is relevant to the lives of ordinary people.*
>
> *Undoubtedly the most dramatic moment in this recent history came when the Roman Catholic Church, virtually overnight, replaced the Latin mass with a polyphony of vernacular languages. Protestant churches, which had eliminated Latin four hundred years earlier, could not now match this dramatic gesture. But in their own little ways they went through similar motions. Both the language of the Scriptures and that of congregational worship were subjected to translations that were supposed to make the message and the proceedings more understandable to the people in the pews as well as more relevant to their lives. In Protestantism, too, there has been*

a turn to the vernacular. But closest in drama to the Roman aggior-
namento *(an apt phrase indeed in this context) has been the radical
revision of the Anglican* Book of Common Prayer, *translating the
solemn Elizabethan cadences of that great monument of the English
language into the antiseptic prose of, say, the British Broadcasting
Corporation.*

*There has been some overt resistance to these moves. Conservative
Catholics travel long distances to a parish where, almost furtively, a
Latin mass is still celebrated. Traditionalist Episcopalians gather
in a dissident congregation for the old service, carefully leafing
through the worn-out pages of ancient prayer books no longer printed
by the denominational presses. There have even been some rather
feeble schisms, reminiscent of the rebellious Old Believers in
Russian Orthodoxy. But very few protests came from the ecclesiastical
intellectuals, most of whom endorsed the vernacular revolutions
with varying degrees of enthusiasm. As to the ordinary people in the
pews, when they were asked (which, and then only rarely, was
typically by pollsters rather than church officials), they said in large
numbers that they disliked the changes. Very few of them organized
in any serious way to resist. Many of them voted with their feet,
quietly slipping away from the liturgies that had been updated for
their benefit.*

*As a sociologist of religion I was already struck at the time of the
Second Vatican Council by the fact that there was little if any
empirical evidence to indicate that ordinary Catholics found the
Latin mass remote or difficult to understand (especially with
English missals in hand). The remoteness and the incomprehensi-
bility was posited* a priori *by theologians and prelates. The same
lack of evidence pertains to all the other programs of vernacularization.
I'm not aware of any studies showing that ordinary people in
England or in the United States had problems with the language of
the old* Book of Common Prayer. *Conversely, there is at least some*

empirical evidence to the effect that many faithful Catholics and other Christians have been put off by the liturgical innovations of the recent past, some so seriously as to become alienated from their church. There is some exquisite irony in this. . . .

This observation is hardly conclusive, but it suggests what may well be the underlying mistake of the vernacularist assumption. It is, to be sure, not the only mistake. There is also the patronizing notion that ordinary people are unable to find their way through proceedings in an unfamiliar idiom—a notion, as noted before, that is almost certainly mistaken when it comes to liturgical language. But there is a more fundamental error in the notion that worship must minimize the remoteness of God as much as possible. To be sure, the error is not total. Of course any form of worship will seek to mediate between the remoteness of the supernatural and the reality of everyday human existence. Of course the Bible, if it is to be read by ordinary people, must be translated into a language that they can understand (far be it from me to disapprove of Luther's great achievement in this matter). And of course it makes no sense for a preacher addressing, say, a German congregation, to speak in Greek. Thus there must be a place for the vernacular in Christian worship. But vernacularism, as it has come to be widely established in the churches, may well be described as a subtle and yet very damaging heresy. It is fundamentally misguided to use linguistic means to deny the transcendent remoteness altogether, to pretend that we can speak of God as we speak of politics or commerce, to try to conceal the divine otherness."

Let us remind ourselves that as some Orthodox begin to tinker and experiment with new "translations" and liturgical innovations, and as some individual priests take it upon themselves to vernacularize or "update" (read "dumb down") the Liturgy, other Christian bodies have been actively engaged in just such experiments for the last forty years. We Orthodox can perhaps learn something from them about where the first small steps

LETTER XVII

of revisionist "liturgical reform" eventually will lead. In the light of recent history, it seems that Professor Berger is absolutely correct (dare I say Orthodox?) in pointing out the fallacies and the ludicrous results of the rush to vernacularize and modernize worship in the West.

We Orthodox should understand that we do not live in a vacuum. The same impulses, often for good motives, that have driven Roman Catholicism and much of Protestantism into liturgical and theological chaos could also overtake us.

In fact, we have seen this happen before. The art styles of the sixteenth-century late Renaissance and nineteenth-century Romantic painters thoroughly corrupted the art of iconography not so long ago. Only now are we beginning to restore the sacred inheritance of the Church in iconography. Do we want to do to the iconography of the language of worship what was done to the painted icon? Do we want to spend the next two hundred years trying to restore what was squandered?

As ever,
Frank

LETTER XVIII

Dear Fr. Aristotle,

Philip Sherrard, it should again be noted, was perhaps the greatest modern translator of Greek poetry and sacred texts into the English language. He writes in *The Sacred in Life and Art* that our infatuation with innovation in art has led to the destruction of true art and creativity. I would like to share a passage of Sherrard's study that is relevant to the issue of the liturgical reforms that are overtaking the English-speaking Orthodox Church in North America.

Professor Sherrard discusses what sacred art is. He points out that in the West the cultural fad that began in the Renaissance of absolute creative freedom and veneration of "artistic genius" has largely destroyed the possibility of sacred art in the West.

Sherrard writes that when creating sacred art, whether this is iconography of the painted or liturgical kind, we Orthodox are to faithfully repeat the Truth, not pretend we can invent "new truths." Moreover, Sherrard shows that all true art is a priestly intermediary between the spiritual realm and ordinary life and that, in this sense, all art, both secular and sacred, is liturgical. Obviously what he writes about sacred art and iconography also has a very direct application to the art of liturgical iconography, translation work, scholarship, and the "art" of the life of the Church.

Sherrard writes:

> *"If . . . art [or translation] is to have life it must come from a union of being with the being whose image his work is to enshrine, just as love can subsist only in the union of lover and beloved. But when a work of art [or liturgical translation] is fully energized in this way—when theme and style are felt and lived—such categories as old and new are meaningless. What is important is not newness or innovation, still less any form of modernity, but the nowness—the immediacy—with which what is always to be expressed is expressed.*

LETTER XVIII

Thus there can be no such thing as an avant-garde *among the artists [or translators] of this kind of [sacred] art, for the simple reason that there is nothing of which one can be* avant *or in the rear. Since this kind of [sacred] art [or translation] is the expression, not of a world of formlessness that for the first time is emerging into form, but of a continuous reality in full formal operation, the only ultimately valid questions to be asked when trying to assess the value of such a work are to what degree has the artist's [or translator's] imagination been informed by the archetypes of this reality and to what extent has he succeeded in communicating his apprehension of them in living terms. Moreover, though there may well be—in fact, inevitably will be—variations in the modes in which individual artists [iconographers or translators] apprehend these archetypes, and so in some measure in their artistic styles, there is absolutely no value, and certainly no absolute value, to be attributed to the new or innovatory as such.*

Concomitantly, in this perspective there can be no such thing as progress or evolution of consciousness in art [or liturgical translation], any more than there can be in life and culture as a whole, seen as taking place along the linear axis of the space-time continuum that we call history. Indeed, one could have thought that the absurdity of the very ideas of progress and evolution in this sense would be quite evident to anyone capable of responding even slightly to the great works of art [or liturgy] which are part and parcel of our inheritance; for there is not and cannot be any criterion according to which it is possible to demonstrate that the artifacts of our modern civilization evince a higher degree of intelligence, beauty or of any other positive quality than, say, an Egyptian temple, the poetry of Homer and the Book of Kells. It would appear to follow that it is only in ignorance of man's artistic inheritance that one can seriously subscribe to ideas of this kind, an ignorance one might expect from scientists but not from those whose ostensible concern is with the arts [or the Liturgy] themselves.

LETTER XVIII

As for the purpose of such an art, [or translation] this is what one might call liturgical. . . . Such an understanding of the nature and purpose of art [or liturgical translations] is immediately eclipsed in one who has no religious faith. . . . As we have seen, the chief of these articles or tenets of faith that [the unbeliever] . . . substitutes for his loss of religious faith [is] a belief in the reality of evolution. The theory of evolution—a hypothesis, like all other scientific theories—is peculiar in that it implies an extreme, if often subtly concealed form of arrogance on the part of those who accept it. By accepting it one is committed also to accepting that theories of understandings held in the past are outmoded, however relevant they may have been in their own time, because human consciousness has now evolved or progressed beyond them. But this is only a covert—and not so covert—way of saying that one is more intelligent or in possession of a greater degree of knowledge than those of the past who formulated or adhered to such theories and understandings. A corollary of this is that one is further bound to assert that no degree of human consciousness or knowledge has been attained in the past which is higher or superior to that attained by the most advanced minds of one's own age. By the same token, failure to invent or subscribe to new theories and understandings, thus demonstrating that one is not in tune with the zeitgeist or with the new state of things now emerging for the first time into consciousness, is tantamount to confessing that one is stereotyped, hackneyed and virtually a museum-piece. . . .

Such a conclusion is of course inherent in the premises from which it develops: that man is no more than an inescapably time-bound, evolution-conditioned being with no immortal soul, and that his art [iconography, Liturgies] and creativity cannot possess therefore any significance other than that which can be formulated quite adequately in hedonistic ('I know what I like'), sociological, scientific, or psychological terms."
(The Sacred in Life and Art, *pp. 50-53)*

131

LETTER XVIII

Is not what Sherrard describes above *exactly* the problem common to some of the new translations of our traditional Orthodox texts into English? Is not the blindness of those who believe in "progress" and "enlightenment" as an inevitable evolutionary phenomena exactly the blindness of Orthodox (or Roman Catholic and Anglican) "translators" and "expert Liturgists" who wish to update and make "easy to understand," "ordinary," "relevant," "sensitive," and "politically correct" material out of the ancient texts of the Church? Above all, is not the spirit of modern innovation that of putting our trust in philosophers rather than theologians who, by Orthodox definition, are men of prayer?

St. Simeon the New Theologian writes:

> *"The Spirit of God is revealed not to the rhetoricians or philosophers, not to those learned in the writings of the Greeks, not to those studying foreign works, but to the poor in spirit and in life, to the pure in heart and in body."*
> *(St. Simeon the New Theologian, Ta Apanta, Thessaloniki, 1969, "I Homily 25," p. 135, trans. by Sherrard)*

We Orthodox believe in the Holy Mysteries and Holy Tradition. If we hold to our Tradition, then is it really such an urgent matter that everything become as modern, "sensitive," "enlightened," "understandable," "inclusive," and "user-friendly" as possible? Is there not a little room in our ancient Church for political *incorrectness*, poetry, and splendid old-fashioned grandeur in how things may be said, not just *what* is said?

Perhaps words like *Thee* and *Thou* and *mankind* that lift our services out of the ordinary contemporary "politically correct" usage are not such bad things after all! Perhaps a little awe and respect is not altogether out of place in the context of the presence of the God Whose essence we cannot describe or understand and before Whose energies we bow. Perhaps we should remember that the unique glory of Orthodoxy is its iconographic sense of the sacred timelessness of God as well as God's incarnational

LETTER XVIII

immanence. Surely in our desire to express timelessness and immanence we must use our own iconic Orthodox liturgical expressions and not borrow from the jaded, politicized hand-me-downs of contemporary Western fashion?

As ever,
Frank

LETTER XIX

Dear Fr. Aristotle,

In my opinion, Orthodox Christians who want to understand where modern liturgical reform will lead would do well to attend a couple of modernized "people's Masses" at any local American Roman Catholic parish. We Orthodox should compare the frivolous, 1960s-style, semiliterate entertainments of modern American "Catholicism" to the Byzantine Liturgy. Such a comparison should be made not on just historic and theological grounds, but on esthetic grounds as well. Beauty matters!

Questions of taste, beauty, and poetry are not irrelevant to Orthodox worship. Moreover, it hardly needs saying, but those Orthodox ecumenists, including some bishops, hierarchs, and others who speak of an eventual Orthodox "union with Rome," would also do well to experience the dreary farce of what post-Vatican II Roman Catholic worship *really is* today. Before trying to force the Orthodox Church's fortunes to be joined to the Latins' sinking ship, we should look at what actual, real-life, fragmented, and political contemporary Roman Catholicism has become, not just at historical Catholicism, theology, and questions of the Papacy, serious as those concerns are.

Orthodox priest, scholar, and convert from Roman Catholicism, Fr. Alexey Young, writes about the harm suffered by traditional Roman Catholics in the wake of the liturgical reforms, not to mention the radical changes, that followed Vatican II. It seems to me that it is very important that we Orthodox grasp the importance of what Fr. Young writes about for two reasons. The first is that we need to know more about the reality of what reform has done to Roman Catholicism so that we can, at all costs, avoid repeating the same mistakes. Second, we need to look before we leap—or are pushed—into a "union" with a fragmented, papal church.

Fr. Young writes:

> *"In 1967 the official Vatican newspaper,* L'Osservatore Romano, *announced that 'liturgical reform has taken a notable step forward on*

the path of ecumenism. It has come closer to the liturgical forms of the Lutheran Church.' Many applauded this development. A few were shocked. . . . Numerous traditionalist organizations have been founded by disaffected priests, nuns, and laymen, all of them risking censure. Some have already been disciplined for refusing to accept the teachings of Vatican II. But those on the 'right' hardly pose a threat to their church. Indeed, they long to return to the days of strict discipline, preconciliar doctrine, and obedience. . . . It is because of the reformers on the left that institutional Catholicism is collapsing. These are far more numerous than the traditionalists, more outspoken, and clearly more influential in all areas of Catholic society. Major changes in liturgy, theology, and world view have caused a committee of Roman theologians to declare that their church is now in 'a period of spiritual crisis that is without precedent.'

This is because of what [noted Roman Catholic writer and ex-Jesuit] Malachi Martin calls the 'dechurching of Christians': 'For almost twenty years now, the churches have been dedicating themselves predominantly, in some cases exclusively, to issues of sociology and politics. They have been led into deeper and deeper commitment to public action of a kind indistinguishable from the local political club. This commitment has changed the way they pray and worship and preach the Gospel. . . . No one knows what will be left intact, or how long Christians of a later generation will have to struggle in order to regain that essential link with the Jesus of history, without Whom Christianity becomes one huge, dead joke.' Let us now examine some of these important changes and their meanings. The primary liturgical act of Roman Catholicism is the Mass. Except in certain conservative religious orders, the concept of the Lord's Supper as part of a whole liturgical cycle (including Vespers and Matins) is now completely lost. . . . For centuries [the] Mass had been heard only in Latin, a language in which most lay Catholics were not fluent. Consequently, when Vatican II authorized

LETTER XIX

*vernacular Masses, changes in the prayers went unnoticed except by
a few who pointed out that doctrine had been changed. For
instance, the offering of praise to the Trinity was suppressed and, in
addition, references to God became vague and deistic. . . .
The dogmatic title Mother of God (in Greek,* Theotokos*) so dear to
Orthodox Christians, and also to Roman Catholics until recently,
was suppressed. Other omissions appear to suppress the doctrine of
the communion of the saints, whose intercession is now rarely asked
(such things being left to the 'discretion' of the individual priest).
Even the words of Our Lord, spoken at the last Supper, were altered
in the 'canon' of this New Mass! Perhaps this is not surprising,
when one remembers that a millennium ago the Roman Church
considered it perfectly reasonable to insert the* filioque *clause into
the Creed, thus altering the doctrine of the Holy Trinity and incur-
ring the anathema of the Nicene Fathers who had forbidden any
tampering with the Creed. . . .*

*Other changes in the prayers of the Mass are too numerous to
mention here. But in general, the whole emphasis was shifted. As
one horrified Catholic priest, James Wathen, observed: 'Of its very
nature, the 'New Mass' 'liberates' the 'children of God' that they
might make a game out of worship. . . . Intrinsic to the very idea of
the 'New Mass' is that the people are more important than Christ
the Savior. . . . Is it not they who must be entertained, accommo-
dated, and emoted over? In the incessantly repeated phrase, 'The
People of God,' it is the people who, in Marxist fashion, are being
acclaimed, not God. . . . They have been given the place of God.'*

*More and more priests are using the New Mass as a 'setting' for
incredible 'events'. To cite one recent example, the Socialist-
Feminist (and pro-abortionist) leader Gloria Steinem recently
accepted an invitation to speak in a Catholic church in
Minneapolis. (She reportedly boasted of the 'momentary delight' she
had 'at the thought of defiling the altar.') One of the guests was a*

LETTER XIX

Methodist layman. He was so scandalized by Miss Steinem's remarks that he left in disgust, saying, 'They might as well invite Satan himself to preach at this church.'

The old axiom lex orandi, lex credendi *(as we worship, so we believe) is certainly true. The desacralized New Mass lends itself to unchristian ideas and behavior. Roman Catholics have now almost completely lost the ascetic spirit. Whereas Orthodoxy still proclaims that the essence of Christianity is asceticism, and to this end gives Orthodox Christians strict fasting rules as a standard for Christian life, Catholicism has almost completely abandoned any such idea. To take fasting before Communion as an example—when I was a child in the Catholic Church, the faithful were required to fast from all food and drink from the midnight before. Later, this was changed to three hours . . . and finally, in the wake of Vatican II, to one hour.*

One Orthodox theologian says this about the Roman Catholic spirit of reform: 'The papal idea, based on the corrupt modern principle of spiritual self-satisfaction, is either to give a special "dispensation" from the standard . . . or else to change the standard itself so that the believer can fulfill it easily, and thereby obtain a sense of satisfaction from "obeying the law". This is precisely the difference between the Publican and the Pharisee: the Orthodox man feels himself constantly a sinner (in spirit if not in letter), whereas 'modern' man wishes to feel himself justified, without any twinge of con-science over falling short of the Church's standard' [Fr. Seraphim (Rose) of Platina].

The German theologian Hans Kung, the most famous of the liberal theologians, now teaches that the dogmatic definitions of Christ's divine and human natures are obsolete: *They must be 'transferred to the mental climate of our own time.' Apparently the 'mental climate of our own time' is Arian, for the Jesuit Piet Schoonenberg*

LETTER XIX

wishes to completely drop all reference to the two natures of Christ, and the Dominican Edward Schillebeeckx says that Jesus was only a human being who gradually grew 'closer' to God. Others now speak of the Savior as 'a man elected and sent by God.'"
(An Appeal to Roman Catholics, *St. John of Kronstadt Press, Liberty, Tennessee, 1979*)

Orthodox hierarchs, bishops, priests, and lay people should be aware that we, too, are not immune from the humanistic and "ecumenical" spirit of the age. This spirit preaches unity with falsehood and peace based on compromise, not Truth. In my opinion, the idea of an Orthodox union with the modern Roman Catholic Church is as ridiculous as the idea that we Orthodox can pursue our own modern agenda of liturgical reform and still have a shred of our ancient faith left intact.

As ever,
Frank

LETTER XX

Dear Fr. Aristotle,

You asked me to substantiate the remark I made to you on the phone last week that there are indications that the spirit of secularism is creeping into the Orthodox community through some of our scholars, translators, and bishops—a few of whom seem to have a weakness for following secular fashions a little too closely. (Perhaps some of them have an unhealthy desire to be accepted and legitimized by their secular academic or social peers.)

It seems to me that a small but influential group of Orthodox scholars on various Orthodox "Liturgical committees" have contracted the secular (often feminist) and vernacularist virus. This is no secret. Their translation work speaks for itself. Sadly they are not alone in their compromise with the spirit of the world. Other Orthodox have also been revising their opinions in the light of modern, politically expedient, sociological, and psychological "discoveries". For instance, there have been several recent instances wherein various Orthodox publications from some of our American Orthodox seminaries have glowingly endorsed books calling for the Orthodox Church to overturn our two-thousand-year-old Tradition in the matter of the ordination of women.

Perhaps out of misplaced ideas about academic freedom (not to mention a desire to "keep up with the times"), formerly stalwart bastions of Orthodoxy, such as St. Vladimir's Seminary, have seen fit to promote and publicize these antitraditional, Westernized views. For instance, feminist Susan Ashbrook Harvey's glowing, uncritical endorsement of the ordination of women in her review of *The Ministry of Women in the Church (St. Vladimir's Theological Quarterly*, vol. 37/1 1993) is only one of several instances wherein the radical feminist theology of self-realization has been given space in an "official" Orthodox venue.

It appears that even some well-known and revered Orthodox bishops have begun to bow to contemporary fashions on gender and related issues. For instance, Greek Orthodox Bishop Kallistos Ware has revised and updated the new edition of his book, *The Orthodox Church*. In his new, revised edition of his book he says that the ordination of women is now an "open question" in the Orthodox Church! Apparently he not only has changed his views on the male priesthood, clearly expressed in the earlier editions of his book, but it seems that he has also misstated the Orthodox Tradition in his newly revised book in favor of a more "politically correct" Orthodox "history". (Other British Orthdox have also called for the ordination of women, for instance, Anthony Bloom. Perhaps there is something contagious about Anglicanism!)

Everyone knows that the Orthodox Church has never ordained women in Her entire history. And everyone knows that this is because God has choosen to reveal Himself as a *Father* and because He sent His *Son* and that His Son, Christ, is represented by the priest as a living icon and that Christ apointed *male* apostolic leaders. Despite the current disingenuous attempt by some Orthodox and non-Orthodox politically liberal and feminist church historians to confuse the role of deaconess and presbytera with that of priest, no serious work exists to substantiate the ordination of women in the historic Church. Certainly no Orthodox scholarly work calling for the ordination of women predates the advent of modern feminism.

The male priesthood has, until recently, been so taken for granted in the Orthodox Church that there has been precious little ever written about this consistent element of the Christian Tradition. Now, ironically, it is just this lack of written dogma that some more "liberal" Orthodox seek to take advantage of in an effort to "prove" that the Church has never had an opinion on this matter. (Given the logic of this approach, perhaps cannibalism was also widespread or an "open question" in the early Church since the Fathers spend so little time denouncing it!)

Today's feminist and revisionist "discoveries" exist only in the modern era. As both the content and overly convenient timing of the new, pro-feminist interpretations of Orthodox Church history show, they are clearly politically motivated and a product of radical chic, not scholarship. Indeed, they are part of a pattern in the academic world wherein first one ancient Christian practice after another comes in for its turn of being debunked.

LETTER XX

The only thing new is to see some Orthodox beginning to play this tired game.

The problem of a creeping, incremental, revisionist invasion of the Orthodox Church is not limited to one or two bishops, seminaries, or feminist scholars. Other signs of looming difficulties abound. Presently there is an effort underway to produce something called the new *Pan-Orthodox Translation of the Liturgy of St. John Chrysostom* (also known as the *Common Liturgy*). This translation work is being done under the auspices of SCOBA, (The Standing Conference of Orthodox Bishops in the Americas.)

To say the least, the first drafts of the new "Pan-Orthodox" translation of the Liturgy are not encouraging from a traditional Orthodox point of view. The first draft of this "Common" Liturgy, as it is all too aptly called, is tastelessly vernacularized, abbreviated, and paraphrased. It uses gender inclusive, politically correct language in slavish obedience to the sort of feminist "guidelines" adopted by the Association of American University Presses. In one draft that is being circulated, there has even been a change in the wording of the Nicene Creed to make it more feminist, more "inclusive"! The Pan-Orthodox translation is about as poetic as the Nynex Yellow Pages. It reads like a second-rate high school textbook. Shakespeare would roll over in his grave, and so would St. John Chrysostom. Chrysostom is not only known for his eloquence, but also for his use of language in its highest poetic and iconic form. The new translation is clearly the work of a committee that knows and cares little for the English language. If something was done in Greek that was this pedestrian and shoddy, there would be a revolution. However, it seems that English is still regarded as a second-class language in some Orthodox circles.

Vigorous protest over the liturgical cloddishness in the new SCOBA translation from many Orthodox quarters has slowed but not stopped the "progress" of this effort. The translation committee has already distributed copies to some Orthodox churches for comment. So far this seems to be nothing more than an effort to get "rubber stamp" approval so that later

LETTER XX

the new Liturgy can be claimed to have been "accepted by the people."

Scholar and priest Fr. John R. Shaw has made a detailed study of this new "translation" of the Liturgy. After a painstakingly lengthy and detailed analysis of its severe linguistic, theological, and esthetic shortcomings, he concludes:

> *"The new proposed translation misses much of the breadth and depth of the [Greek] original. In short the translators were: 1) not seeking Orthodox unity, 2) nor presenting a witness of the Faith (note the proposed feminist change in the Creed!), 3) nor [making a] correct translation, 4) nor preserving the wisdom of the Church's tradition, 5) nor even using particularly good English.*
>
> *The only clearly evident goal in this piece of work seems to be liturgical reform, some of which could be a major source of scandal to anyone raised in Orthodox tradition. Its introduction [into the Orthodox Church] could only lead to further polarization, and probably to schism."*
>
> *(Fr. John R. Shaw,* Reflections On the Proposed "Common Liturgy Translation," *Milwaukee, 1995)*

Father Patrick Henry Reardon calls the SCOBA translation, "a pitiful progeny of a faddish conjunction." It is quite evident that, left to themselves, some of the well-meaning liturgical "experts" involved in this SCOBA translation project are quite prepared to do to the Orthodox today what the Anglican and Roman Catholic "experts" did to their brethren in the 1960s and 1970s. The cloud of liturgical reform, the size of a man's hand, is on the Orthodox horizon. The question is: Do the bishops of the Church know or care about what is being done in their name? Are the bishops being intimidated by their "experts" and scholars? Do enough Orthodox know, care, or understand what is at stake? Will we take a stand against the corruption of the English language edition of our sacred Liturgy? (See Appendix for a more complete and entertaining analysis of

LETTER XX

the SCOBA translation by Patrick Henry Reardon.)

Perhaps none of this should surprise us. Remember that an ideologically motivated attempt to secularize the Orthodox Church, particularly the Greek Orthodox Church, is unfortunately not a new phenomena. A consistent and, unfortunately, successful effort has been made in Greece by political leaders of a secular, Westernized, humanistic persuasion (since the revolution of the 1820s) to secularize and Westernize the Greek nation and, by extension, the Church. For instance, the Enlightenment humanist Adamantios Korais, who was the philosophical father of the revolution of 1821 and 1822, attempted to secularize the Greek Church in the nineteenth century and to "update" it in accordance with the nationalistic principles of the French Enlightenment. Korais even thought that the Greek Orthodox Church should be forced to collect money for his state-sponsored secular and humanistic education programs. (Korais' effort is somewhat reminiscent of what happened in Russia as Peter and Catherine worked so hard to Westernize and modernize the Orthodox Church of the eighteenth century.)

What took place in nineteenth-century Greece is perhaps similar in some ways to the present attempt to secularize Orthodoxy in North America from within through the agenda of liturgical reform masquerading as "translation." Perhaps we should learn from the results of what happened after the Greek Orthodox Church became partially subordinate to secular and humanistic Westernized scholars following the Greek nation's liberation from the Turks.

Professor Sherrard writes:

> "A breach [was] opened between the higher clergy and the Greek peasant people which [left] the latter exposed, in a way that might not otherwise have been so devastating, to the impact of the new [humanistic] spirit; in other words, the teachers [academics] took the place of the clergy as the intellectual directors of the people. The result was a considerable confusion and bewilderment. . . . The

LETTER XX

> *slow breakdown of the religious conscience of the Greek people, and of the whole manner of life based upon it, in the name of the ideas of a 'hellenism' imposed from without by educators who, whether they knew it or not, were merely the representatives of a West-European culture in a most degenerate form, is a drama whose final stages have not yet been completed."*
> (The Greek East and Latin West, *pp. 178-79)*

Just as some Greek scholars and political thinkers of the eighteenth and nineteenth centuries imported French Enlightenment humanism and French ideas about nationalism into Greece (ironically in the name of a resurgent Hellenism!), so today some of our contemporary Orthodox academics are apparently eager to import Western "enlightened," "sensitive," and "inclusive" egalitarian feminist utopianism into the Orthodox Church. The vehicle that they have chosen is one of liturgical reform and historical revisionism. Translation work is a mere excuse, a convenient "cover" under which to do covertly what they would not dare to do openly. Moreover, these "experts" know perfectly well that the bishops are too busy to give their revisionist work much close scrutiny and that the common people trust their leaders and will generally accept what is given them. In this ruse, this abuse of trust, they have not been original, but merely copied the technique of the leftist and humanistic secular Knowledge Class who have so effectively taken control of our national debate by seizing control of our language and our history. This is not to say that I believe that all the translators on the SCOBA committee are consciously trying to undermine the Orthodox Church. On the contrary, I am sure they are doing what they think is best. The problem is that what they believe to be best for the Church seems to be a series of incremental reforms intended to update and modernize Orthodox worship. They seem embarrassed by our so-called high church tradition and seem to want to make our worship more "Protestant" by using vernacular, common English in a way that makes our Liturgy common and ordinary. They are not alone in this linguistic and ideological crusade. Certain Orthodox groups have openly been pushing a reformist, modern liturgical agenda

LETTER XX

for several years now, as have a number of academics in our seminaries.

Fr. Aristotle, let us not be naive. American and British Orthodox academics have had to labor long and hard in the intensely secularized, feminized academic vineyard to receive their degrees. Few people are immune to their environment. We all get tired of being the odd man out. And none of us, least of all myself, do very well at resisting the temptation to conform to the age and environment we are in.

We all desire to be accepted and liked. We all would like to be on the "right side of history." And we all make sinful compromises. Since we are all sinners, it is very difficult to criticize Orthodox brothers and sisters, particularly bishops and priests. One wants to be respectful, humble, and obedient. But at times we must speak out. We have no choice. Teachers of Orthodoxy, particularly liturgical translators, seminary professors, historians, and bishops, are in a unique position to do a great deal of lasting harm to the Orthodox Church. It is our duty to stop them when we believe them to be wrong. Unfortunately, what they do they do in a public forum, so it is in public that they must be challenged. None of us have the right to expose the private sins and failings of others, but once a public stand has been taken, written, or taught (for instance, in a seminary class, history book, or liturgical translation), then we must stand up and publically correct the error as best we can.

Given the apparent desire of some Orthodox to conform to the ecumenical, utopian, egalitarian environment, extreme caution is in order when dealing with any Orthodox translations or theological/historical works of scholarship that have even a whiff of political correctness about them. We cannot be silent about these issues if we want to see the Orthodox Truth passed on to another generation.

The conciliar tradition in the Orthodox Church should begin with this prayer:

LETTER XX

*"Put not your trust in princes, nor in the son of man, in whom
there is no help. His breath goeth forth, he returneth to his earth;
in that very day his thoughts perish."*
(Psalm 146:3-4)

It seems clear when our leaders, scholars, and even bishops begin to echo the secularizing spirit of this world, they are indeed putting their trust in princes. However hard it may be to do, we cannot deny our responsibility to speak out.

In the book of Acts we read of a very different reaction to the spirit of the world on the part of the Apostles than that of some of today's Orthodox leaders. When the Apostles were confronted by attempts of their "Knowledge Class" to force them into politically correct behavior, they stood up to them and refused to bend. After Peter and the Apostles were freed, following their arrest and appearance before the Sanhedrin, they prayed: "Now, Lord, behold their threatenings; and grant unto thy servants, that with all boldness they may speak thy word" (Acts 4:29).

It seems that it is the lack of boldness in answering the challenges of our "Sanhedrin" that is costing us so dearly. In view of this, we must ask why changes in Orthodox Liturgy, history, theology, or Tradition are now being made, suggested, or "discovered". Is it because these changes better reflect the teachings of the Fathers and the original Greek language of the Liturgy, or is it because they consciously or unconsciously reflect the academic and political fashions of the passing moment? For instance, one wonders what new information about the teaching of the Fathers has come to the attention of Bishop Kallistos Ware regarding the ordination of women that was not available to him *before* the advent of the modern feminist movement? And one wonders what facts the translators who want to vernacularize the Liturgy have discovered to show that the vernacularization of worship in other religious bodies has been a good thing?

As ever,
Frank

LETTER XX

P.S. I close with an excerpt from an article in the *New Yorker* magazine, ("Scripture Rescripted: In a New Version, the Bible Goes P.C.," by Anthony Lane. October 2, 1995) for your edification and amusement.

How ironic that the *New Yorker*, hardly known as a bastion of Orthodox thought (!), justly mocks the absurd linguistic, feminist shenanigans of some particularly lame "biblical scholars" for the very same linguistic sins that some of our Orthodox scholars now seem so eager to commit.

"These are dark days, if you happen to be God. Not only are the peoples of the earth writhing in sin, as per usual, and taking your name in vain, but some of them are wondering whether your name was the right one in the first place. The New Testament and Psalms: An Inclusive Version' (Oxford; $14.95) gets itself into a dreadful pickle over the precise etiquette of worship. Like a teenager who doesn't know what to call his friends' parents, the editors of this brave new project are torn between shyness and presumption in the face of a superior being. 'God' will do, but 'Lord' is a no-no, because it reminds us of iniquitous social hierarchies. 'Master' is even worse. As for 'King,' well, forget it. No one that closely involved with the male-monarchical-military complex is going to make them drop to their knees.

The editorial board of the Inclusive Version is composed of six American experts. . . . Their joint beef is the conviction that an entrenched terminology is blocking our access to the Almighty. Words that are sticky with racial, sexual, and physical prejudice have bleared our vision for too long. Clear the pathway, therefore, and we shall see God, for the first time, in all His glory. Correction: in all God's glory. The pronoun 'His' suggests a masculine presence, whereas the true deity is neither male or female—it encompasses and goes beyond both to find a higher, genderless perfection, like RuPaul. The problem for the editors of the Inclusive Version is that they have a much nicer time finding fault than correcting it. Their solution to the sex conundrum, for instance, may not enjoy quite the universal appeal that they intend:

LETTER XX

'Our Father-Mother in heaven, hallowed be your
name, Your dominion come.'

I guess that, over the years, those intoning the Lord's
Prayer could learn to junk 'kingdom' (with what the editors call its
'blatantly androcentric and patriarchal character') and speak
instead of 'dominion.' But will they ever come round to 'Father-
Mother'? In my view, the moment critique for this unwieldy phrase
comes in the second chapter of Luke, when Jesus [is] missing and is
found by his worried parents—his mortal father and mother— in
the temple: 'Jesus said to them, 'Why were you searching for me?
Did you not know that I must be in the house of my Father-
Mother?' But they did not understand what Jesus said to them.' I bet
they didn't. . . .

We should not only deplore the literary wrecking of the Gospels but
also escape the insidious danger of treating them simply as litera-
ture—the idle prerogative, to be blunt, of unbelievers. It is no coin-
cidence that the strongest prose, at once the most compact and the
most capacious, ever produced in England should have risen at a
time when society was most tenaciously rooted in the faith. There
was a world within the Word. That is one reason why the King
James Version, born largely of Tyndale and published with the
encouragement of James I in 1611, has endured, and why subse-
quent efforts to update it, or to dump it altogether and start again,
feel doomed from the start: no one can pretend that our language
hasn't changed (and change need not always mean decay) but
neither can one deny that under social pressure it has peeled away
from religion. Trying to stick it back is futile; and the effort to
claim 'relevance' for any version of the Bible smacks of sheer
historical vanity—a delusion that the word of God should somehow
try to keep up with us, crank itself up to our level rather than the
other way around."

LETTER XXI

Dear Fr. Aristotle,

You say you agree with the points I raised in my last letter, but some people might say that I that make too much of a fuss over several "minor problems." You may well be right. Perhaps I am just allergic to the idea that we need a "new and improved" Orthodoxy. Perhaps I have been more impressed by the holiness of the "old-fashioned" monks, nuns, and grand-mothers I have met in the Orthodox community than by the scholarship of some of the up-to-date Orthodox leaders I have met.

Some people might say regarding "minor" changes in the translation of the Liturgy or other religious texts, "what difference can a few small changes make? Why make such a fuss over such a minor thing? Who cares if the Liturgy is poetic or beautiful or not?" Or they might say, "Bishop Kallistos Ware is so wonderful in all he does, such a wonderful spokesman for Orthodoxy, why bother making such an issue over one minor error of judgment regarding his change of opinion on the matter of the ordination of women?" Well, Fr. Aristotle, I have some thoughts on what are "minor issues" and what are not.

When I was eight years old and on vacation with my family in Portofino, Italy, I received a tiny, very minor, almost invisible, cut on the little toe of my left foot. At the time I was swimming in the limpid water of the Mediterranean. I hardly felt my toe lightly brush the mussel shell that scratched me. I paid the injury no mind until the end of the day. When I showed the small cut to my father he said, "Never mind, it's nothing; it's only a minor scratch. The salt water will have cleaned it out."

At three in the morning my father was proved very wrong. You see, he did not know that the water where I had been swimming was near an open sewage pipe. The water I had been swimming in when I cut my foot would not have been fit to clean out a gutter! It looked clean, but its pure, turquoise beauty masked an inner, unseen reality.

My "minor" scratch became seriously and instantly infected. At

LETTER XXI

3:00 a.m. I woke with a raging fever of 105 degrees. (I still remember the deliciously delirious sensation of floating around my room!) My leg and foot were swollen to more than twice their normal size. Only the swift action of my parents and a doctor (and large doses of penicillin) saved my life.

My "minor" cut was not the problem. The problem was the *environment* in which I received the wound.

The "minor" changes we see in the liturgical language of the Church, the "minor" vernacularizations, the "minor" edits, the "minor" gender inclusive use of new terminology, the "minor" historical revisions on the male priesthood, are not taking place in a pristine, antiseptic vacuum. These changes are being made, or at least proposed, in the context of the desacralized, polluted waters of the secular and humanistic twentieth and twenty-first centuries. They are being proposed in the same historical environment in which major Protestant bodies have been thoroughly corrupted and destroyed by "liberal" theology. They are being made in the context in which the Roman Catholic Church has abandoned its own historical traditions (Vatican II) and become a mere shadow of its former self.

The twentieth century is not religion-friendly or even religion-neutral. Never has traditional religion received more brutal harassment than in our era. This is the era of Stalin, Mao, and Hitler. We are the children of Turgot, Voltaire, Rimbaud, Freud, Darwin, Descartes, Picasso, and Nietzsche. This is the world built on the hatred of God. America is the country that has stripped the Ten Commandments from our schoolroom walls and forbidden prayer in schools. This is the period of history in which feminism has unleashed a revisionist war against the English language and against all hierarchy and tradition. This is the era wherein a holocaust has been launched, in the name of "feminism," "choice," and "rights," against women and babies via the abortion trade. Easy "no-fault" divorce and the worship of careers at the expense of children has become the norm in our day for both men and women, not the exception. This is the world in which our academic elites have pitted themselves mercilessly

LETTER XXI

against those with traditional views in a coercive "politically correct" crusade against tradition, hierarchy, and belief in absolute moral standards. This is the day and age in which liberal Roman Catholic and Protestant theologians have colluded to strip the Bible and the Christian Tradition of its sacramental value and its historic trustworthiness. This is the world in which the very idea that Truth can exist has been denied and in which religion has been reduced to a subjective, internalized, psychological experience.

It is in the highly poisonous climate of the late twentieth century that the "small" wounds in the body of the Orthodox Church are being made, often by well-meaning or naive people who have no idea of the magnitude of what they are doing. These same people look toward the twenty-first century as a period of even more change. It seems that some of our priests, hierarchs, theologians, scholars, translators, bishops, and bureaucrats have no idea of what they are swimming in. They may indeed be learned specialists in their own fields, but this does not mean that they understand the wider cultural *milieu* they are inhabiting.

We believe that the gates of Hell will not prevail against the Orthodox Church, but this does not mean that our part of the Church (for instance, the Orthodox Church in North America) cannot become thoroughly corrupted and eventually disappear. Something worse could even happen to us. The Church in North America could survive as a "false" Orthodox Church.

It seems to me that no particular jurisdiction or Patriarchate, let alone an individual priest, bishop, or hierarch, is guaranteed perpetual authority. It is the Church Herself and the office of bishop and priest that are perpetual, not individuals. The Orthodox Church will survive, but, who knows, the day may come when Her only faithful bishops are in China or Mexico or in lands that have never even heard of Orthodoxy at this time. Ancient sees of the Church have disappeared into the sands of time before, and they will again.

LETTER XXI

It seems to me that old buildings, vestments, and long, white beards an Orthodox do not make. It is what we *do* that counts. Orthodox hierarchs, bishops, and priests have no authority in themselves outside of the Holy Tradition. If their faithfulness to that Tradition waivers, or is corrupted, their authority evaporates, no matter how much pomp and circumstance they are surrounded with, or what titles they have, or how ancient the see they serve. This is the Orthodox way.

We must not confuse respect for the office of bishop and priest with our ultimate duty to do whatever we can to preserve the integrity of the Orthodox Church and the Truth that dwells in Her. The monastic tradition of humility and obedience becomes twisted into a mere excuse for cowardly silence if it is used as a reason to avoid our responsibility to speak out when the Truth is at stake. Remember the tradition of the ancient Church: When a bishop is ordained, the people call out *"Axios!"* (Worthy!) to signify their approval. However, the people also had and have the right and *duty* to call out *"Anaxios!"* (Unworthy!) when a false candidate presents himself. It may not be as pleasant to call out *anaxios* as *axios*, but then, being a responsible grown-up is not always fun.

As ever,
Frank

LETTER XXII

Dear Fr. Aristotle,

In answer to your question about why so many supposedly God-fearing Americans accept, or at least tolerate, legal abortion, here are some thoughts. I believe we Americans have learned to live with abortion as a means of social engineering because to admit to ourselves what abortion really is and what it does to babies would be to spoil a good time. Remember that the most common American greeting is Have a nice day!

Having a nice day is the fulfillment of our modern American dream. We do not wish ourselves a blessed day or a holy day or sinless day, but a nice day. We are so determined to not spoil a good time that we are quite prepared to work very hard to blunt our moral sense in order to drown out the inner voice of conscience that might make us feel guilty about something—the casual practice of abortion, for instance.

Feeling guilty, especially if you have no intention of repenting, is the opposite of having a nice day. Admitting that you live in a country that sanctions the cruel and capricious murder of one-and-a-half million innocent babies a year tends to wipe the grin off one's face. Abortion must be "okay" because we do it so often, and we're such nice people, aren't we?

In order to have a nice day in a not-nice world, it is necessary to be sentimental but not virtuous. That way we can feel good about ourselves without having to change our behavior. That way we get to have our cake and eat it too!

The same hospitals that have doctors in them engaged in a search-and-destroy mission for handicapped babies (through amniocentesis and abortion) have handicapped ramps for born children. The same hospitals in which seven-month-old babies who fail an amniotic test are dragged from their mothers' wombs have reserved handicapped parking spaces. The parking spaces are for people with the same handicaps that the children who are aborted are condemned to death for. They are killed when their parents and doctors discover, through amniocentesis and other eugenic, genetic screening procedures, that they are less than "perfect," less than nice. The only difference between the aborted child and the child in the wheelchair using the handicapped access ramp is that one is a few months older than the other. If you are nine months old or younger, you can be killed. If you are nine months old or older, you have a parking space reserved for you. "How can you say I am a coldhearted eugenicist? Look at the cute little girl using our handicapped access ramp. I treat her, too!" Sentimentality is a great comfort to the truly wicked. (Remember how Hitler loved his dog, Blondie?) "I've helped thousand of women have babies. I've only done a few abortions!"

We Americans delight in sporadic public convulsions of sentiment, but we are not in the business of sacrificial compassion for the long haul. Suffering is not nice. It's not fun.

Remember how we stopped work and play a few years ago when a little girl fell down a well? Remember the moment-by-moment television coverage of the rescue operation? Remember the national outpouring of joy when the toddler was rescued? Remember the close-ups of the fireman's begrimed, tear-streaked face?

But who cares to remember that during the day that we held our breath over the fate of eighteen-month-old Baby Jessica, that we aborted four thousand other three-to-nine-month-old babies? Who cares to remember that the same people who give to the Jimmy Fund support a federal government which pays for cruel experiments on living and dead aborted babies in fetal research? (President Bill Clinton signed the executive order permitting government funding of this fascist atrocity within forty-eight hours of taking office.) And who cares to remember that thousands of children become orphans of the divorce courts as we parents pursue our "American dream" of self-realization, lust, and avarice and discard our children like the wrapping from a piece of half-eaten fast food?

Why do we kill our unborn and neglect our born? It is for the same reason that we refuse to discipline our children who survive. We deny reality because reality is not always nice. We deny the true nature of man because it is inconvenient to contemplate it. We deny the facts of life because the biology of childbearing gets in the way of a good time. We do this because we live in a haze of self-contradiction and sentimental negligence. One can have a nice day every day only if one denies reality.

America's answer to Auschwitz is to build Disneyland next to it. America's answer to rude, uneducated, mannerless, neglected, undisciplined children is to purchase them video games. America's answer to broken families is weekend visits. America's answer to a failed educational system is to buy desktop computers for each illiterate thug-in-training, hoping that pretty pictures and cartoons will bribe the young visigoth to read diminishing amounts of text. America's answer to violence in schools is to install more metal detectors and to hire more security guards. America's answer to minority low "self-esteem" is to falsify history textbooks and to lie about how *profound* primitive, pagan cultures are. America's answer to crime is to build more prisons. America's answer to unsafe streets is to shop by mail-order catalog so that there is no need to even leave one's home and venture out into the mean streets of downtown USA. America's answer to the chaos created by the so-called sexual revolution is abortion.

How can you have a nice day if life becomes cluttered with responsibilities, sacrifice for others, and selflessness? How can you have a nice day— every minute of that day—if you have to spank your children when they are naughty, teach them to read, hold them on your lap, lay aside career ambition and stay home with your family, teach children by example about what is right and wrong, live a holy life of self-denial, fast, pray, go to confession, change the content of your character, be silent and hear the voice of God, treat the earth and its creatures with respect and love, live modestly as part of an ascetic struggle for holiness, and seek each day to have a sinless day and sinless night? Does this sound *fun, nice, self-fulling,* or *uplifting?* Does it even sound American? Is *this* the pursuit of *happiness* the founders of our amusement park guaranteed us?

LETTER XXII

We are too busy having a good time! We are too busy working to get ahead! We are too busy to stay near our grandchildren! We are too busy driving all over the continent in our motor homes *enjoying* our retirement! It is more fun to take our children to Disneyland than to discipline them, love them, teach them manners, and read out loud to them. Saying no is such a drag! Just turn up the TV instead!

How can you have a nice day if you're pregnant with a baby you don't want? How will you ever become a vice president, a regional director, or an air force captain with a fat bellyful of "genetic tissue" and engorged breasts full of milk?

How can you have a nice day if you have to have sex with your same old wife when her flabby thighs and stretch marks don't look like the playmate centerfold you have taped up over your workbench in the garage? How can you have a nice day if you have to send those child support payments to those brats and that bitch in Muskegan, Michigan, now that you've moved to L.A. and found a nineteen-year-old with a perfect ass? Didn't you already send them a Nintendo video game? Didn't you take them to Epcot Center? Who says you're not generous? Didn't you give to the United Way? Didn't you send thirty cents a day to the Christian Children's Fund and get some cute letters and crayon pictures back from your "child," cute little Lopez (or was it Pedro?), until you moved to Houston and lost the address?

Who are all these bastards who are yelling about child support, anyway? Aren't these the same creeps you saw at Woodstock and in Haight-Ashbury thirty years ago preaching *free* love? Aren't these the same feminists who you saw on TV twenty years ago demanding the benefits of *no-fault* divorce? Aren't these the same psychologists you saw on *Donahue* ten years ago extolling *uninhibited* self-expression? Aren't these the same women you saw on *Oprah*, talking about the joys of *single*, male-free motherhood?

Real education takes discipline. Real love takes discipline. Real marriage take discipline. Real life takes discipline. Real spirituality takes discipline. But discipline is not fun. Discipline is not nice. Discipline is not American. Self-denial has no place in our expanding vocabulary of "rights."

Self-discipline is not even constitutional! The Supreme Court has ruled that the Constitution guarantees the "right to privacy." The first rule of the right to privacy is that we Americans are free to do what we please in private and, er, well, in public, too! Right?

So pump up the volume, sail that boat, play that golf, drive that dirt bike, play that CD-ROM, download that Internet porno file, camp in that national park, chase that career, abort that baby! *You deserve to be you!* Have a nice day!

As Ever,
Frank

LETTER XXIII

Dear Fr. Aristotle,

In answer to your last letter, it seems to me that there are three insurmountable problems regarding an Orthodox union with Rome. Unfortunately, many Orthodox seem only to be aware of the first of these.

(1) The particular historical differences between Rome and Orthodoxy related to the Schism which culminated in A.D. 1054 were the *filioque*, as well as papal supremecy and claims to universal jurisdiction.

(2) The fundamental and profound theological, liturgical, and philosophical differences between the Latin West and Greek East lie at the heart of all the East-West disputes. Our two very different worldviews amount to a profound difference in the way reality and Truth are perceived. The West trusts reason and dogma. The East trusts divine mystery and the individual's intuitive spiritual intellect to which Truth is revealed by grace through a process of ascetic struggle. The West concentrates on what one *believes*. The East concentrates on what one *is*. To the West worship is an intellectual, creedal exercise. To the East worship is the heart of theological expression and leads to communion with God. The West *studies* the Scriptures. The East *prays* them. The West trusts human authority to lead the Church. The East trusts the Holy Spirit and the priesthood of all believers.

(Our profound differences with the West are rooted in the Western legacy of the rationalistic Roman empire and Aristotelian philosophy. Our differences are also rooted in the Western, Augustinian idea of the division between body and soul and the utter "fallenness" and "depravity" of mankind called "original sin.")

(3) Negotiating union with the Roman Church of today (post-Vatican II) is not even to negotiate with the historic Western church. It is to negotiate with a rapidly moving target. In truth, the Pope no longer represents the fragmented, divided Roman Church (except on paper and on television) any more than one Protestant leader represents all Protestants. The mod-

LETTER XXIII

ern Roman Church of "one billion Catholics" is in total chaos. The loudest lament for this chaos is expressed by conservative Roman Catholics themselves.

Today's Roman Catholic Church contains Marxist liberationists, traditionalists, feminists, liberal theologians, New Age "charismatic" Catholics, and a whole range of nominal believers in various states of rebellion against Rome and the historic teachings of the Western Church. As the saying about Los Angeles goes, "There's no *there* there!"

It seems to me that the Orthodox who are negotiating with Rome in order to achieve a "union" hardly understand the first point mentioned above, that is, the particular historical differences between Rome and Orthodoxy. They have ignored the second point: the fundamental divide between the West's faith in Reason and the East's belief in the process of divinization through ascetic participation in the sacramental life. And as to the third and most practical point, the actual state of Roman Catholicism, we hear nothing. As a result, the false impression is created that our differences with Rome are merely rooted in a set of obscure, possibly irrelevant, theological "differences" and several historical "misunderstandings" that belong to another place and time.

The possibility that we are close to union with Rome is astounding. How can we have union with an entity that is in chaos and which can no longer realistically even be defined as one church? One might as well negotiate a treaty of "union" with the seventy-five thousand tribes of Africa! With whom will we have union? the Pope? the liberal theologians? the liturgical reformers who have literally demolished the ancient Western tradition of worship? the laicized, rebellious, Marxist religious orders? the Roman Catholics who wish to return to pre-Vatican II tradition? the secular-humanistic Jesuits who barely tolerate the present Pope? the European "liberal" theologians?

On the ground, so to speak, the relevance of both Rome and Constantinople is incidental to ordinary Roman Catholics and Orthodox.

162

LETTER XXIII

The present Pope is beloved, but the Orthodox would not, however, unite with the present Pope but with an evolving, disintegrating assemblage, loosely called the "Roman Catholic Church." The average Orthodox would not travel to St. Peter's to participate in a papal High Mass but would be trying to figure out his relationship to the local, desacralized, modern Roman Catholic parish in his neighborhood.

For the individual Orthodox, union with Rome would bring nothing but confusion. Will he keep the fasts of the Orthodox Church any longer? (The Roman Catholics do not; indeed, many do not fast, *period*!) Will he go to confession? (Most Roman Catholics do not.) Will his wife, daughter, and children serve the Eucharist? (The Roman Catholics allow women, children, and passersby to both serve and receive the Eucharist.)

Some Roman Catholics might say that, according to official canonical, liturgical rules, what I have written above is not true. For instance, that the new post-Vatican II role of the "Eucharistic server" is strictly guarded and requires special training. However, as anyone even vaguely familiar with modern American Catholicism knows very well, the point is that the rules are not being kept. They are being ignored wholesale. This wholesale Roman Catholic rebellion against the canons of the Roman Church is in contrast to the Orthodox Church, which, in spite of our own share of scandal, does not have sacramental and liturgical chaos swirling about its altars. Compared to the Roman Catholics, we even appear downright orderly in our liturgical unanimity. Ironically, it is within the "chaotic" Orthodox community that we find sacramental purity in comparison to the liturgical, desacralized chaos of the authoritarian, "organized" Roman Church.

In contrast to Rome, it is clear that the glory of the Orthodox Church has been Her genius in simultaneously maintaining apostolic succession, Holy Tradition, absolute faithfulness to Her liturgical tradition, and the autonomy of Her bishops. What the Roman Catholics for centuries derided as chaos (remember, they used to call us the "withered branch" of Christendom!) has in fact been a magnificent balancing act of unity within

LETTER XXIII

diversity. Without knowing it, much of the world is trying to find ways to imitate the Orthodox genius for this unity within diversity.

Today the Roman Catholic Church and the humanistic ideologues who are calling for unity of all Christians, in the name of "saving humanity" and "world peace," are out of step with reality. We are in a new era. The old Marxist, leftist, utopian ideals of collectivism, central planning, and socialism are being discarded. They are being discarded because they do not work. From the collapse of the Soviet Union to the failure of the American Federal welfare system for providing solutions to alleviate poverty, we see the bankruptcy of centralization as a means of human organization. From the failure of the United Nations' peacekeeping initiatives to the failure of the so-called mainline denominations to keep their members, we learn that the old utopian idealism about unity at any price and one-world government has died.

Dictatorship and central planning committees are "out" and freedom and local autonomy are "in." International bodies such as the League of Nations and the United Nations, whose prestige was derived from eighteenth- and nineteenth-century Enlightenment ideals of humanism and collectivism, are now thoroughly discredited.

The only people who pretend to believe in utopian collectivism anymore, or Enlightenment or Romantic movement ideals, are a few overpaid bureaucrats at the United Nations and the World and National Council of Churches, whose lucrative careers depend on the humanistic philosophy of collectivization as the only *raison d'être* for their parasitic careers. The only other true believers in the notion that centralized power will produce the brotherhood of mankind are a few leftists scattered throughout some Western universities.

But wait! There is one other obscure elite group of out-of-touch ideologues and bureaucrats swimming against the tide of diversity, decentralization, local autonomy, and freedom—the ecumenists of the Orthodox and Roman Catholic Churches. Only they still seem to be true believers in

LETTER XXIII

the idea that collecting millions of people into one, centrally governed and controlled megagroup is a good idea. These hierarchs and a handful of Orthodox and Protestant ecumenists and the bureaucrats who run the discredited, failed, and woefully out of touch "League of Nations" of religion—the World and National Councils of Churches—are the last people on earth who seem to believe that human problems can be solved by signed declarations of unity and by consolidating the authoritarian power of bishops and hierarchs into a "one-world government" of Christianity. Their slogans about "one-and-a-half billion Christians" uniting in "fraternal love" could have been written by the old hacks of the 1930s Communist party, except the word *Christian* is used instead of *workers*. Now that these ecumenist ideologues have been joined by the Pope in his call of union with the Orthodox, the circle is complete. The Roman Church wishes to do with talk of love what it failed to do with its armies, but the universalistic, authoritarian principle is the same. Napoleon would approve.

This curious phenomena is not surprising. The impulse of Rome has ever been to bring the world under its sway. It has been in love with "order" since it cut its first deal with Pippin and the other Germanic emperors. The Roman Catholic Church has always had ridiculous delusions of grandeur. (Who else could have produced Baroque art or the modern papal road show—circus—media event!?) But what is surprising *is* that the Orthodox, who *invented* the idea of the local *autonomy of each bishop,* should fall for this universalistic, humanistic, collectivist nonsense.

Where have the Orthodox ecumenists been living? Have they missed the major lesson of the twentieth century? Have they failed to understand that the movement of history is *away* from centralized and false aspirations of unity for unity's sake and toward local autonomy? Do they know that the roots of the twentieth century's utopian love affair with unity, centralization, and globalism are in the Enlightenment and Romantic movements, and that these philosophical movements were built on a hatred of Christianity by people like Jean-Jacques Rousseau?

LETTER XXIII

That Roman Catholics should be in love with a capable and charismatic Pope is understandable. John Paul II is a wonderful, even admirable, man. But whence comes this Orthodox ardor for Rome, for union, for globalism? What Orthodox could think that human social problems could be solved by politics? What Orthodox could believe that unity is the creature of official declarations rather than shared beliefs? In fact, what Orthodox could believe that the peace of Christ is equivalent to the world's idea of "peace," or that humanist unity is the road to salvation?

Surely the Orthodox view is that human problems are the result of sin, not bad social policy? Surely we Orthodox, of all people, should be rejoicing in the world's recognition of the ancient Orthodox principle that true unity only comes through a conciliar and shared commitment to ideas and tradition, not through "top-down" official declarations and political alignments? And surely the duty of any Orthodox bishop is to preach change of heart and change of life through ascetic struggle, not salvation through grandiose, papal-style political schemes? The present Pope may believe that all roads lead to Rome, but surely the Orthodox should know better!

The difference between Orthodox Christians and Roman Catholics is that integral to Roman theology is a belief in the Papacy. If the Pope decides to seek unity at all costs, he cannot be stopped by his own people because he *is* the Roman Catholic tradition. (When, in 1870, Pope Pius IX was about to proclaim the dogma of papal infallibility, he was reproached by some cardinals who said that this was "contrary to Tradition." The enraged Pope shouted: *"I am Tradition!"*) For Orthodox believers, however, Tradition is not vested in a man but stands apart from those who guide the Church. Orthodox Tradition has its own identity.

The Roman Catholics can remain within their tradition while obeying the Pope. We would have to deny our Orthodox Tradition in favor of an ecumenical unity built on the compromise of Orthodox principles. This is a very bad bargain. This "unity" will achieve nothing more than damaging the Orthodox Church. This type of "unity" is a top-down affair, not truly grass roots. There will only be official declarations, not a shared purpose. It smacks of coercion, not conciliarity.

LETTER XXIII

It seems that the failure of the League of Nations, the United Nations, and the World and National Council of Churches (or Napoleon, for that matter) to realize any of their lofty Enlightenment-era "brotherhood of man" aims should teach us a lesson. The lesson is that true peace and unity can only be a spiritual by-product of the unity of a shared, voluntary commitment to first principles.

Do we Orthodox truly share the ideas and first principles of modern Western philosophy embodied in *today's* Roman Catholic Church? I believe not. Do we subscribe to the humanistic revolution that has shaped the post-Vatican II Roman Catholic Church? I believe not. Will the Roman Catholic Church truly rescind the institution of the Papacy? I believe not. Then what, except good feelings, photo opportunities, and meaningless mutual declarations of undying love, will our "unity" be based on?

                    As ever,
                    Frank

LETTER XXIV

Dear Fr. Aristotle,

Thank you for your letter. Let me clear up a point you raised. Of course I am not saying that just because we should reject Enlightenment-humanist notions of ecclesiastical unity with the Roman Catholics and Protestants that this means we should not work with other Christians.

Of course we should join forces with any person or group that might be regarded as a fellow traveler with us on a whole host of issues. But there is a vast difference between the authentic unity of a shared purpose—say in standing up for the right to life of the unborn—and the false, forced, bureaucratic-humanistic type of "unity" that is the product of official declarations and lofty utopian ideology.

On a human level, a local level, and on the level of individual issues as they arise naturally, we should work with anyone who is "going our way." It seems to me that this is in the spirit of Christ's words that he who is not against us is for us. Indeed, we should go further. It seems to me that we must humbly admit that there are many Roman Catholics, Protestants, and others who, as individuals, are on a far more consistent and holy path toward Christ than us.

We must reiterate that while we Orthodox believe the Church is indeed the Orthodox Church, we also believe in the mystery of the mercy of God transcending even the boundaries of His Church. This being the case, it seems that we should work with many people of many creeds for the common good. But all of this is a far cry from calling for ecclesiastical unity as if the Orthodox Church can negotiate a "middle position" between Truth and error.

Strangely enough, we Orthodox, on an individual basis, often have more in common with some conservative, traditionalist Roman Catholics and conservative Protestants than we do with some of our own worldly-wise "liberal" bureaucrats. This is because shared belief, on whatever level, is always a stronger tie to bind people together than "official" pronouncement. It is the difference between the authenticity of a grass-roots movement and State propaganda from the top down. It is the difference between the practical unity that is achieved when neighbors work together in a good cause and the irrelevant declarations of politicians.

An Orthodox monk pursuing Christ in his ascetic struggle may well have much more in common with a devout, Protestant pro-life activist who has endured the mocking hatred of a pro-death world than he does with some "official" Orthodox representative to the humanistic and liberal World Council of Churches. The Athonite monk and the American Protestant activist would understand each other if they met. Both put Christ first, at great cost to themselves. The Protestant pro-life activist may not call his hard road an ascetic struggle, but we Orthodox believe that God honors the intent. The nonviolent pro-life activist in his jail cell has a lot more in common with the monk in his monastic cell than he does with the leaders of his own Protestant denomination as they sit at a long conference table discussing church politics.

A good marriage is not based on the ornate wedding feast or the priest's pronouncement of unity. A good marriage is based on daily contact and a shared commitment to first principles of practical love and forgiveness. Divorce courts are full of people who have signed prenuptial agreements and who were married by judges, pastors, and priests. The marriage license—the piece of paper—is worthless. From a human perspective, a shared commitment to ideas is the only glue that binds.

For us Orthodox, it is *because* we remain true to our Tradition that we can freely collaborate with many non-Orthodox in many ways. From feeding the poor to stopping abortion, from working against secularism in our colleges to revamping our educational system, there are many areas where we can collaborate with the non-Orthodox. But the need to work with others is, it seems, very different than the utopian idea that somehow we can all be "one". It is as different as a man who has a good marriage and many good friends who happen to be women, and a man who decides to marry all the women of the world in order to bring about world peace! There is a difference between adultery and friendship, not to mention common sense and utopian insanity!

Collaboration in a good cause or because of a shared principle, while reserving the right to recognize differences of opinion, is a good thing. Thinking that we Orthodox can "become one" with all varieties of Christianity is as silly a notion as that expressed by the sorts of misty-eyed utopians who sincerely believe that if everyone would just hold hands and sing, "We Are the World," that somehow a new age of fraternal love would begin.

If we want real unity between all Christians, we should concentrate on Orthodox evangelism. We should explain the good news of Orthodoxy and invite all those who profess Christ into the fullness of the One, Holy, Catholic, Apostolic, and Orthodox Church.

The loftiest human intentions often create the worst disasters, because human beings are sinful. The lofty ideals of the humanistic French Revolution ended in the guillotine. What a contrast with English history! England has no written bill of rights, but rather has a strong commitment to individual liberty that has preserved the genuine rights of man. France enjoyed all the declarations one could want and yet had a bloodbath. The English had a tradition of individual liberty but no "official" piece of paper. Who was better off?

Just because sensible people reject utopian, collectivist notions about the unity of all Christians—the kind of "unity" that is favored by popes and Orthodox ecumenist bureaucrats—does not mean that a practical unity between like-minded Christians or a unity of shared purpose is a bad thing. The problem is that bureaucratic unity, like all diplomacy, is neces-sarily built on falsehood. Politically negotiated "unity" brushes authentic differences under the carpet in order to achieve "oneness". But this one-ness becomes an awful thing. It mocks the idea of absolute Truth by mini-mizing the religious claims of not only the Orthodox, but of conscientious Roman Catholics and Protestants as well. This is the type of "unity" that

LETTER XXIV

Roosevelt, Churchill, and Stalin agreed to at Yalta. It is the kind of "unity" that the African tribes have killed each other over ever since some idealistic and greedy white European bureaucrats arbitrarily drew the African borders to "consolidate" all the tribes.

If history teaches us anything, it is that we should fear grandiose, utopian schemes by our leaders. Most to be feared are schemes for world peace, unity, and consolidated power in the name of the "good of mankind."

As ever,
Frank

LETTER XXV

Dear Fr. Aristotle,

You wrote asking how I would explain the need for spiritual self-discipline to a young adult group. Well, invite me to speak at your church and see! In the meantime, the following thoughts may prove helpful.

A firebreak, as you know, is a line cut in a forest by firemen fighting a forest fire. They clear the forest and brush far ahead of the holocaust, in order that the flames will have nothing on which to feed. There is no use cutting a firebreak next to a fire. By the time you have felled the trees, dug up the earth, and cleared the brush, the fire will be upon you and will roar over you into the trees beyond. The only way to make a firebreak work is to cut it well ahead of the fire, taking into account the direction the prevailing winds are blowing the flames and sparks. Moreover, you have to cut the firebreak wide enough to stop the wind-driven flames. A narrow break is of no use at all.

Above all, the firebreak must be thoroughly prepared. *All* the brush, timber, leaves, and dead wood must be cleared out or the flames will find fuel and jump the break.

A firebreak only will work if the firefighter does not try to save the entire forest. A large piece of the forest will have to be sacrificed in order to salvage the rest. This sacrifice will involve not only the trees destroyed by making the firebreak, but also the trees abandoned to the flames between the break and the advancing conflagration.

It seems to me that the same principles are at work in our spiritual lives as in fighting a forest fire. The flames are our passions. The wind that drives them is the spirit of the age. In order to fight our passions and the spirit of the age, it is no use resisting the flames at the actual site of the fire. At that point resistance is futile. It is too late.

The wise Orthodox Christian will set up "firebreaks" well ahead of time, in anticipation of the never-ending battle to guard the verdant forest of our innermost beings. As with a physical firebreak, there is no piece of dead wood too small to matter. In addition, the firebreak between our passions and the world's spirit must not be narrow. It must be wide or the flames will jump the trench. In this regard, even the "small" details of life that require a measure of spiritual self-discipline matter. They may not amount to much in themselves, but they matter a lot in the context of clearing the dead brush in order to build an effective break between the world's spirit, our unruly passions, and ourselves.

Let me give you an example. Headcoverings for women in church are now considered old-fashioned and outdated in most North American Orthodox communities. Yet some of the same people who might laugh at the idea of women returning to the ancient Orthodox tradition of wearing headcoverings in church also lament the loss of modesty and chastity in their own daughters and granddaughters. Now, obviously, wearing headcoverings in church will not magically cause people to be modest and chaste. Nor will headcoverings prevent men from lusting after women. Nor are they salvific or a major element of Orthodox life. Nevertheless, our grandparents (not to mention the Apostle Paul) were not stupid.

Our forefathers and foremothers understood that symbolic gestures often have large consequences. Outward actions teach inward habits. They teach us to see the world and life in a certain way. They teach us to become certain kinds of people.

I believe that the small "old-fashioned" details of Orthodox life add up to a big firebreak. These things are not magical or even mandated (they form a rule of life, not a law), but the old firebreak is a sensible way of contributing to a *general atmosphere* of Christian life that helps us keep the Commandments and seek divinization.

We do not learn how to live as Christians—in other words, how to keep the Commandments and the Beatitudes—from the Bible, rule books, or from "big" or "important" actions only. Often it is in the multitude of small details that the habits of daily life are learned. Headcoverings, for instance,

LETTER XXV

not only teach modesty, but also respect for God. This object lesson of respect, awe, and modesty in the face of the otherness of the Holy is not only for women. Men, too, learn from being in a church in which women have taken the trouble to cover their heads. The modesty of Orthodox women teach Orthodox men by example. We men are reminded that church and worship are special, different, apart from mundane life. We are reminded that the things of God are to be approached with fear and trembling.

Who can say what creates an atmosphere of reverence? I certainly can not. But I do know that it is the details of a thing that combine to produce a total effect. I know this from my own experience as a movie director. I know this as a novelist. And I know this as a father.

We should ask ourselves a question: What makes it easier, rather than harder, for Orthodox Christians to live holy lives in our desacralized world? In other words, what are the details of worship that encourage Orthodox habits of life?

The idea of creating an atmosphere that is conducive to a moral life is behind many "minor" externals practiced by the Orthodox Church. The Church, in Her ancient wisdom, has encouraged us to practice certain good habits for millennia. For instance, take our habit of making the sign of the cross. This habit is not a meaningless reflex. Since body and soul are one, what the hand learns to do the soul will learn also. If we wish to teach ourselves and our children a sense of awe and respect for God, then we must teach them to make their cross at the names of the Trinity, the Theotokos, or the Saints. This "small" action builds a "firebreak" between the flames of carelessness and thoughtlessness and the Orthodox faithful. Moreover, the cross actually contributes to our salvation. The cross is no mere symbol, but the bridge between God and man.

The necessity to have good physical habits of worship is one reason that the addition of pews into American Orthodox churches is such a tragedy. Pews prevent us from worshipping with our whole being since they hinder us in making prostrations and in circulating freely to venerate the icons. Worship is not education, entertainment, or a "mental attitude." Worship is the *whole person* entering into reverential, loving communion with God.

Clearly good habits set the tone for all of life. The man who has the habit of standing up out of respect when his wife enters the room is less likely to strike her in another context. Manners, civility, courtesy—these things are not minor at all. They form the intimate texture of authentic human life.

It seems that the road to barbarism, in all spheres of life, begins not with big actions but with the incremental abandonment of the small courtesies of civil discourse. The Germans broke the windows of Jewish shopkeepers long before they gassed them. In America, sexuality was reduced to the status of a contact sport a decade before abortion was legalized.

Before becoming a prostitute, a woman must first lose her sense of modesty incrementally. Before sleeping with various men for money, she must first change the way she dresses, acts, and thinks about herself.

The man who beats his wife begins by being rude over dinner. There is the first time he slaps her, then the first time he punches her. Perhaps he waits for the sky to fall. It does not. Then he punches her again. Soon it becomes "okay" because it becomes frequent. We can get used to anything. It has been said many times that the worst feature of wickedness is its extraordinary banality.

We do not lose our faith overnight, but gradually. Perhaps we forget to keep our morning rule of prayer for a day or two. Suddenly a week has past in which we have not been in our prayer corner before the icons. Then weeks become months, and finally years.

Now let us consider some of the "petty details" that some Orthodox say do not matter anymore in our churches. Perhaps some priests are willing

LETTER XXV

to regard letting these "details" fade away as a necessary matter of "economy." Perhaps they believe that they should become more up-to-date. Perhaps they begin to vernacularize the English version of the Liturgy. God is no longer addressed as "Thou" or "Thee," but as "you," as in, "Hey, *you*, c'm' 're!" The altar boys are allowed to be later and later in putting in an appearance at Liturgy. Less and less people come to confession. First the headcoverings go, then miniskirts are worn to church. We men stand behind women, contemplating their figures, not the prayers of the Church—let alone God, Christ, or the Theotokos. At Holy Week a "new translation" is used that is, in fact, an edited text. Bits and pieces of ancient prayers are missing from this "translation." Well, if these can be cut, why not other things? If there is no appropriate standard of behavior in church, why should there be one in any other part of life? If the priest is so busy trying to be everyone's best friend, who will be their father?

The picture is clear: All that is needed to utterly corrupt the Orthodox Church and Her worship practices is the passage of time combined with the attitude that "Only the big things matter, so why make a fuss over the details?" This attitude will erode everything we call sacred. This erosion does not begin dramatically. It begins with allowing the "small," "silly," "old-fashioned" traditions to quietly slip into disuse, as quiet as an old grandmother lying in her coffin. It begins with the idea that we "live in more enlightened times," that "things are different now," that "what was good for our grandparents won't work in America," that "we should fit in."

I have found that the "firebreak" principle applies to raising children, as well as to life in the Church. (My daughter is now married, I have two grandchildren, one son in university, and my youngest son is a foot taller than me. So perhaps I may be permitted a little fatherly introspection!)

Raising children well and having a good Christian marriage are not activities that can be achieved in separate compartments. One feeds off the other. In both ventures one does well to remember the old saying, "Begin as you mean to go on."

LETTER XXV

In my experience, the battle to raise God-fearing, polite, civilized, responsible, pleasant, creative, literate children is not won or lost in the "big things," but in the daily "minor" details of life. Modest, chaste daughters are produced by loving, modest, chaste mothers who act and speak as they mean their daughters to. Honest sons are raised by fathers who tell the truth to them, including admitting and apologizing for the times that the father makes a mistake (for instance, after being unjust or too harsh). Boys who see their father express respect and love for their mother will learn how to treat all women with respect. Children who grow up in a home where parents read good books out loud to them, and to themselves, will learn to love books. The family that is not self-disciplined enough to sit down together for a daily meal, uninterrupted by television, the radio, friends, or the telephone, is not going to be self-disciplined enough to demand good behavior of the children in the "big things" in life either.

A father that laments that he cannot control his fourteen-year-old's television-watching habits probably lost the battle by using the television as a "baby-sitter" when the child was three. Children do not begin by watching MTV for five hours a day. They begin by watching *Sesame Street* when their parents are too lazy, career oriented, or preoccupied to be real parents.

Of course I know that what I have written above is not in any way a set of absolutes. Nor is everything black and white. Nor are there any magic formulas to raising children or to worshipping in a truly reverential manner. Nor are parents entirely to blame for their children's behavior. But, nevertheless, far too much is being squandered in church and family life among the Orthodox. The most frequent excuse is, "Well, these are only small traditions, these are minor details. Economy demands compassion for people living in our new world," or, "Let's make things a bit easier. We don't want to drive our young people away."

It is a terrible and destructive thing when compassion is employed as an excuse to stop building firebreaks around ourselves, our parish, and our children. Soon small slippages lead to large, life-changing lapses. Soon the very shape of family and church life is irreparably altered.

LETTER XXV

We are weak. We all can be blown this way and that by the spirit of the age. We all need to admit that we need to dig a trench around ourselves.

Big things do indeed matter most. But all big things have small beginnings. All huge conflagrations begin with a single spark.

As ever,
Frank

APPENDIX

THE NEWEST LITURGICAL MONSTROSITY
by Patrick Henry Reardon

Father Patrick Henry Reardon is a priest of the Antiochian Orthodox Christian Archdiocese, serves as pastor to St. Anthony Church in Butler, PA, is an associate editor of Touchstone *magazine in Chicago, and teaches philosophy, social studies, and German at the Community College of Allegheny County in Pittsburgh. Formerly a professor of New Testament and Greek at Nashotah House Episcopal Seminary in Wisconsin and a professor of Old Testament and Hebrew at Trinity Episcopal School for Ministry in Pennsylvania, he did his theological studies at Southern Baptist Theological Seminary in Louisville, KY, St. Anselm's College and the Pontifical Biblical Institute, both in Rome, and St. Tikhon's Orthodox Seminary in South Canaan, PA. In his spare time Father Pat is working on the first English translation of St. Ambrose's commentary on the Gospel of St. Luke, and he has been assigned the translation and notes for the book of Exodus in* The Orthodox Study Bible.

One day nearly a decade ago, during a period when I was slowly groping my way out of the Episcopal Church and towards the True Faith, one of my major mentors in the process, Father Vladimir Soroka, a very talented and devout priest whom I revere and trust, chanced a remark that startled me. Observing that the various Orthodox jurisdictions in this country employed liturgical translations that varied a good deal among themselves, he expressed the hope that the Standing Conference of Orthodox Bishops in the Americas (hereafter SCOBA) would someday establish a translation commission to iron out the differences and present a uniform translation for all those jurisdictions.

I did not respond openly to this suggestion at the time, but I felt a genuine tremor at hearing it. My experience as an Episcopalian had made me very skittish on such matters. At that point in my life I was not disposed to trust ecclesiastical commissions of any sort, and liturgical commissions least of all. We Episcopalians were surrounded by heresy and perversion, and it always seemed to me that the worst heretics and the craftiest perverts invariably got appointed to commissions of some sort. I had already witnessed the ravages inflicted on theology, decent English, and even basic morality[1] by the Standing Liturgical Commission of the Episcopal Church, that nefarious group responsible for the so-called *Book of Common Prayer* of 1979 and the subsequent "trial liturgies" that are occasionally inflicted on the bone-weary Episcopalians to this very day.

I knew only too well the evil works of ecclesiastical commissions. My experience had left me in no doubt that Father Dracula would inevitably be in charge of the diocesan blood drive. I vaguely and unreasonably hoped, I suppose, that the Orthodox Church would eventually declare liturgical commissions a species of heresy, so my first inner reaction to Father Vladimir's comment was a prayer that he would not repeat it to anyone else.

APPENDIX

VERBAL ICONOGRAPHY

After all, there were no obvious problems with the Orthodox translations to which I was most exposed, those of the Orthodox Church in America (hereafter OCA) and the Antiochian Archdiocese. Indeed, I really liked them. Taking their cue from Florence Hapgood's great work,[2] they followed in general the cadences, tone, style, and the very words—even whole sentences—familiar to me from the Coverdale Psalter, the Douay-Rheims Bible, the traditional and authentic *Book of Common Prayer*, the King James Bible, and our better religious poetry as exemplified in, say, George Herbert.

To me this was important. Although in private I daily pray Matins and the Little Hours in the more ancient languages of the Church, each evening my family prays Vespers together in English, and our parish congregational worship is entirely in the vernacular. Now the only suitable English I've found for those times is that inspired by the sources I just listed. Although no human language is worthy of discourse with God, some language is better for the health of the soul, and the history of English recognizes a special style of address for prayer, a style more stately and yet more intimate. It is obvious to me that one does not address God in a style and tone determined by profane and secular usage. This principle is as valid for language as it is for music.

"Street English," in particular, is not an a proper medium for Orthodox worship, any more than electric guitars are suitable for our music, electric light bulbs an adequate substitute for candles, or large photographic posters appropriate for the iconostasis. Ever since the labors in translation by Saints Cyril and Methodius, it has always been recognized that the language of worship must be consecrated. It should not be simply the speech of the marketplace. This insight was implicitly assumed as a principle by those responsible for our first Orthodox translations into English. Br. Isaac Melton put the matter well: Liturgical language, the sacramental word, is nothing less than verbal iconography. A verbal icon, that is to say, a liturgical text, like any other icon, must be holy—it must be set apart by respect-inspiring boundaries. The many and varied veils and covers used in Orthodox worship, from the iconostasis and vestments to the chalice veil and the curtains on the Royal Doors, at one and the same time both reveal ("re-veil") and conceal, thereby eliciting our reverence. The verbal icon must also be "veiled" — it should be decently and appropriately clothed in excellent poetic and artistic language.[3]

Indeed, is it not a point of genuine irony that those earlier generations of Russian and Syrian translators, many of whom probably spoke our own tongue as a second language, had so well captured the spirit of traditional liturgical English? As a newcomer to Orthodoxy, I found the phenomenon genuinely refreshing. Since Anglicanism's loss of the traditional *Book of Common Prayer* in the early 80s, those who have worshipped in the

APPENDIX

parishes of the OCA and the Antiochian Archdiocese are arguably praying in more devout and elegant English than any other religious group in the United States.

A DEGRADED ENGLISH

I was convinced, moreover, that ours is a very bad generation in which to undertake new translations of traditional texts. Right now the English language is energetically and systematically debased nearly everywhere in this country—by government, on television and radio, and most of all by the academic world. Especially relative to this last, I know at first hand whereof I speak, having lived so much of my life on campus. Watching progressive editions of various standard textbooks in English composition, history, philosophy, anthropology, sociology, and comparative religion, I have seen the language in all of them subjected to highly politicized reforms in recent years. The so-called English employed in contemporary college texts and the mandatory use of which is literally forced on both faculties and students bears ever less relationship to the living language of real people outside the academic world. I had no doubt that the next generation of liturgical translators would be drawn from the same academic milieu that is currently killing our mother tongue.

Had I more contact with the Greek Orthodox parishes at that time, there would have been even greater reason for misgiving on my part. In 1985 Holy Cross Orthodox Press released a new translation of the Divine Liturgy made by members of the faculty of Holy Cross Seminary. I purchased a copy of it five or so years ago, and I would have seen some real signs of trouble in its pages, had I bothered to look at it more closely. Not only did that translation abandon the liturgical language traditional in English worship, it even made a significant move in the direction of "politically correct" vocabulary. Specifically, it had intentionally omitted any translation of the words *tous anthropous* from the Nicene Creed. Consequently, the latter now said that the Incarnation was effected, not "for us men and for our salvation," but simply "for us and for our salvation." Not only did that alteration represent a blasé attitude toward the wording of the authoritative Creed, but it was a sign of (at the very least) some shallow thinking within the faculty of Holy Cross Seminary. Indeed, had I checked out the credits listed in the front of that book, I would have found among the its contributors the name of a well-known radical feminist author.

Well, I did not do any of these things. On the several occasions that I served Vespers, Matins, and Divine Liturgy in Greek parishes, whether as deacon or as priest, I invariably did so in Greek, without even consulting the English on the facing pages. Thus, until very recently, I was unfamiliar with the English translation used in Greek congregations for the past ten years. A merciful Shepherd, so tempering the wind to the shorn lamb, spared his frail servant several years of anxiety.

APPENDIX

THE ROMAN CATHOLICS

In fact, however, prior to the Holy Cross translation, prior also to those sad developments in academia— indeed, even before the Episcopalians committed liturgical hara-kiri in the 70s — the liturgical degradation of English had commenced in a big way within the largest Christian body in America. If anyone wanted to learn the evil art of liturgical vandalism to its utter limit, the Roman Catholic authorities in this country had already set the standard and written the rules. The language used in the Roman Catholic Mass in the United States nowadays is incredibly banal. In the 60s the episcopally appointed translators produced English liturgical versions so trite, so irreverent, that I believe their wiser forebears would have dispatched them, promptly and quite properly, to the stake. Oh, where was Torquemada when they needed him?

No other group in America has been so tried by sustained torture as the Roman Catholics in this matter of translation. My son and daughter being educated in Roman Catholic schools, I occasionally find myself attending Mass as part of some scholastic event, and the experience borders on martydom. It is a high testimony to the patience and holiness of the Roman Catholic faithful that they endure it. The sublime and stately cadences as old as Gelasius, the finely balanced constructions of the Leonine collects, words of uplifting majesty dear to Ambrose, and hymns bringing tears to the eyes of Augustine, are now secularized and trivialized beyond recognition. You can hear more reverent English over the public address system at Kmart.

The Roman Catholic translations in this country are so dispirited and lackluster that I have checked out the original Latin of some of them just to make sure. I limit myself here to one horrendous example chosen as random. In Eucharistic Prayer III of the Roman Missal, published by the Vatican, there is a very pure and stately clause that reads: ". . . ut a solis ortu usque ad occasum, oblatio munda offeratur nomini tuo." This brief but theologically rich text is based on Malachi 1:ll, which Christians from the very beginning have read as a prophecy of the Holy Eucharist.[4] A literal translation preserves much of its simple dignity: ". . . that from the rising of the sun to its setting, a clean oblation may be offered to thy name." Instead of that plain and elegant rendering, the translation foisted on Roman Catholic Americans reads: ". . . so that from east to west a perfect offering may be made to the glory of your name." Thus, within mere seconds of being told "lift up your hearts," the faithful out in the pews are then obliged to listen to a sort of TV pronouncement. "From east to west," indeed; it sounds more like a weather report than a prayer. How do people put up with that?

APPENDIX

FEARS AND HOPES

But back to the story. As I came into Orthodoxy, I began to learn a new trust that I had not known as an Episcopalian. Sunday followed Sunday, but I never once heard heresy from the pulpit. Not a single time did I read of an Orthodox bishop questioning the Virgin Birth nor an Orthodox priest blessing a homosexual "marriage." I discovered that moving from Episcopalianism to Orthodoxy is like switching from mud pies to Klondike bars. Attending gatherings of the Antiochian clergy after my ordination, I found them to be experiences in no way comparable to their counterparts in the Episcopal Church. I did not, as formerly, come away depressed, discouraged, sick at heart, and wondering how it was that the gates of hell were prevailing.Then, during the year after my Chrismation, there appeared *The Liturgikon*, a priest's and deacon's handbook of the major services of the Church, translated by Archmandrite (now Bishop) Basil (Essey). This Antiochian version, commissioned by Metropolitan Philip (Saliba), left nothing to be desired, as far as I was concerned. Except when serving in other jurisdictions,[5] I have used it exclusively since ordination. It is a model of its kind and should have been regarded as the norm and standard for any future SCOBA translation. So when, from time to time, there was talk of a joint Orthodox translation of the Divine Liturgy, I became less anxious.

To be sure, I occasionally noticed eccentric clergy, as well as lay seminary professors, with weird ideas. All things considered, the indications were slight, I suppose, but years trying to survive as an Episcopalian had rendered my senses acute, even painfully so. And some things seemed just not right. There were small but recurring bits of evidence, for example, that the liberalizing trends of the east coast academic establishment were seeping into both of our seminaries in that region. For instance, female seminary students were going around to preach on Sundays in northeastern parishes, as though they were training for the pulpit.[6] There was a priest up north who even tried to use girl acolytes.[7] There was also a priest down in northern Virginia who regularly printed an off-beat parish editorial at which I think his bishop could do well, on occasion, to take a closer look. Among other things, he likes to quote bizarre, mean-spirited comments from a monk in New York whose mantia deserves to be yanked from time to time.

But, weighing all things, I believed and still believe such individuals to be rare, and I came to hope their sort would not serve on any liturgical translation commission. I also hoped that any forthcoming SCOBA translation would stand in the classical tradition of English prayer. I further hoped that it would be free of contemporary ideological biases, sociological fads, and general jargon. I hoped, likewise, that the Church would be spared a secularized and eccentric exercise by hothouse "experts."
Alas for those hopes.

APPENDIX

THE NEW TRANSLATION

The Orthodox Joint Liturgical Commission was established by SCOBA four years ago. I became aware of its existence a year later when I received a proposed draft of its work sent out to Orthodox clergy for comment and criticism.[8] In spite of my own immediate and serious reservations about the text, I did not respond right away, out of a newcomer's sense of diffidence.

Then, at the Antiochian Archdiocesan Convention in Pittsburgh in 1993, the two Antiochian members of the commission, Fathers Michel Najim and Edward Hughes, jointly chaired a discussion session that dealt with the commission's work. This was very helpful, for it enabled me to voice my considerable misgivings within the fairly safe circle of brother clergy. I was encouraged to find that my sentiments were shared by most of the priests present, while Fathers Michel and Edward, both of them wise and kindly men, urged me to put my observations in writing and send them directly to the commission. Within a week I did so.

I heard nothing else for two years, except a rumor that an Orthodox theologian and writer, a well-known seminary professor whom I admire, had seen the later version of the translation and found it all right. That news was reassuring.

Then, this past summer there were more disturbing rumors afloat about the latest working draft of the SCOBA translation. It seemed that some parishes were already using it as a field experiment. At the beginning of August I was privileged to serve Divine Liturgy with two eminent hierarchs of the Church, who later discussed the translation with me at breakfast in tones and terms of pronounced unhappiness. Over the next few weeks I requested and received copies of the latest working draft and found the bishops' distress entirely justified.

As a husband and daddy, a parish priest, college instructor, and associate editor of a quarterly magazine, I'm afraid that I do not have the leisure to comment on the latest edition of the SCOBA translation in the detail I should like. The lion's share of my observations is directed to what I regard as the translation's major flaw: the clear, unmistakable intrusion of sociopolitically motivated linguistic reform into the very wording of the Divine Liturgy. This intrusion, which I propose to identify and document, is unconscionable.

I simply cannot imagine what in the world those translators thought they were doing. Their task was to find a reasonable adaptation of the currently used translations so that we would all be using the same formulas. Instead, they came up with an ideologically slanted version alien to most translations now in use.[9] If a major purpose of the new translation

186

APPENDIX

was to enhance our unity, then why produce a work certain to be divisive? I predict that, if adopted by the bishops of SCOBA, this new Rolling Stones rendition of the Divine Liturgy will be the most divisive thing to hit Orthodoxy since the Russian Revolution, polarizing us beyond anything in living memory. Truly, Father Dracula has been put in charge of the diocesan blood drive.

I am confident, however, that the bishops of the Orthodox Church will rise to their duty and completely reject this pitiful progeny of a faddish conjunction. This translation is not only a tragedy; it is also a potential scandal to the "weak brethren," those many Protestants and conservative Roman Catholics who are at present examining Orthodoxy in hopes of finding a new home for themselves and their families. If only for this cause, I cannot imagine its being adopted by the jurisdiction I know best, the Antiochian Archdiocese. A major reason for the continuing phenomenal growth of the latter[10] is its manifest resistance to the corrosive influences of contemporary American faddism, to which SCOBA's new working draft translation is a conspicuous and groveling capitulation.

In my opinion, it will not suffice to touch up the translation here and there. Perhaps it should not even be sent back to the same commission that produced it; indeed, I suggest that the latter be sternly summoned to repentance. This translation is wrong in its very suppositions and conception. It is so deeply flawed as to require a *sanatio in radice*. That is to say, the ax should be laid to the root of the tree.

THE MAJOR PROBLEM

The most disturbing feature of this working draft is its plain sympathy to "politically correct" language. Indeed, it introduces that sympathy into the sanctuary of the Nicene Creed itself, and it does so on the very point of the Incarnation. Hitherto we Orthodox have expressed our faith in one Lord, Jesus Christ, "who for us men and for our salvation came down from heaven, and was incarnate of the Holy Spirit and the Virgin Mary and became man." Regrettably, no more. The word "man," you see, appears twice in that sentence, and "man" fails to pass inspection of today's academic though police, so it must go.

Thus, the commission's new wording is: "who for us and for our salvation came down from heaven and was incarnate of the Holy Spirit and the Virgin Mary and became human." That is to say, we are not "men," nor is Jesus a "man." The same torture is logically applied also to the Monogenes; whereas the older translations say that God's Son "became man," the new version has it "became human." An identical change must likewise be effected in the long prayer of the Great Entrance: "you became a human being without change or alteration."[11]

APPENDIX

Did our revisers intend to change the faith? I really don't think so. Does their revision on this point endanger the faith? I doubt it, at least for now. What they have done, rather—the deed that I find most offensive and strenuously object to—is introduce an academic, secular, ideologically driven formulation of socio-political theory into the holy place, an abomination of desolation standing now where it ought not. This alteration of just a few letters I regard as so egregious an evil that I propose to deal with it at some length. I announce this up front, lest some of the following comments appear to form a digression.

I commence by invoking a Latin adage: *qui potest plus, potest et minus*: "One who can do more, can also do less." Our translation commission took an enormous, unwarranted liberty in substituting "human" for "man" in the Creed and leaving the other mention of "men" untranslated. Having done more, they may now also proceed to do less. A commission that felt free to say "human" instead of "man" will have no trouble saying "visually challenged" instead of "blind," or "hearing impaired" instead of "deaf." This is no joke. Anyone who has watched the march of *soi-disant* politically correct language in the past decade or so will recognize that I do not exaggerate by even a hair.

The Joint Liturgical Commission obviously thinks of itself as enlightened. On the basis of a shaky theory that I plan to impugn a bit later, they have already gone messing with the Nicene Creed. But why stop there? Let's really get busy and raise our social consciousness. Are we Orthodox not aware, for example, of the hostility we unconsciously display to left-handed people by saying that Jesus sits at God's right hand? So let's change that. And what about the liturgical calendar? (Just what we need right now—a new calendar crisis!) Look at those Sundays before Lent: the Publican and the Pharisee, and the Prodigal Son. All guys, not one female. And how is it that only one of the Sundays in Lent is dedicated to a woman? Let's even that up a bit!

As for the Sundays of Pascha, they are almost worse. Thomas gets his Sunday before the Myrrh-Bearing Women get theirs, and then the Paralytic gets a Sunday before the Samaritan Woman does. How can we newly enlightened Orthodox countenance such rampant prejudice? And then the next Sunday is named for the Blindman, who obviously must now become the Visually Challenged Person. Finally, the following Sunday is dedicated to the Fathers of the First Ecumenical Council. Such Neanderthal sexism. So let us reform ourselves; lo, our bold translators have blazed the trail before us.

If the Latin adage is right—if "one who can do more, can also do less"—then there is absolutely nothing now to prevent our making changes on all these things, once we have laid audacious hand on the Nicene Creed. Indeed, some suggestions are already being offered. At a women's workshop at St. Vladimir's a few years ago, an attending *matushka* complained that the Virgin Mary was the only female on her parish's ikonostasis, noting that this relative underrepresentation of women in that holy setting made her feel non-affirmed. Well, a proper pastoral solicitude compels us to affirm that lady, so let's send St.

APPENDIX

John the Baptist packing and tell St. Herman of Alaska to hit the road. Why be meek on such matters when our translation commission has shown itself so brave on the matter of the Incarnation? It has not only pointed out the way to go; it has taken a giant leap in that direction. The rest should come easy.

EXTREME VERTICAL REVISION

Now what I believe truly significant about this development will be clearer if we examine the two ways in which this so-called politically correct language tends to operate in contemporary liturgical revisions. These two ways may be described as vertical and horizontal.

Vertical revision looks to language pertaining to God. It consists in modifying liturgical references in order to balance or neutralize the resoundingly masculine titles by which God has traditionally been invoked or referred to: Lord, Father, Son, King, and so forth.

A more radical form of vertical revision consists in introducing feminine names and titles in order to "provide equal time" to God's softer side, as it were. Examples of the latter effort include the new Methodist service book and the various experimental liturgies sometimes inflicted on those long-suffering Episcopalians. In these revisions God is invoked by names like "Father-Mother," and attention is directed to the fact that "wisdom," one of the titles of Jesus himself in the Christian faith, is a feminine word in Hebrew, Greek, Syriac, Latin, and many other languages.
Such radical revision of liturgical language is necessary, we are told, because so many women nowadays feel alienated by the partiality traditionally shown to masculine nouns, pronouns, and images when speaking of God.[12] Merely as a point of sociology, I'm afraid, this assessment is not chimerical; such women really do exist. I have met plenty of them, especially among Roman Catholic nuns, female Protestant seminarians, and Episcopal priestesses.

However, such complaints tend not to receive a sympathetic hearing among Orthodox women in general, and emphatically not from the Orthodox nuns of my acquaintance. There does not appear to be any danger, at least in the foreseeable future, that Orthodoxy will be tempted to change its liturgical language in a way sufficiently radical to accommodate this extreme form of feminism.

Nonetheless, those women rendered uncomfortable by references to God as Lord, Father, and so forth, may occasionally pose something of a pastoral problem, even for the Orthodox priest. Without necessarily passing moral judgment on the individual state of soul of those thus troubled and trying to speak as politely as one can on this matter, I am

APPENDIX

nonetheless persuaded that such discomfort, considered objectively, is at least a serious temptation, if not a sin, against the Christian Faith. Thus, I am unable conscientiously to alter the counsel that I publicly proffered on this matter five years ago:

> There remains, of course, the pastoral problem of how to minister to those (men or women) who find all this offensive and "very unfair." However this be done (and I doubt that a sincere call to conversion and repentance would be always out of order), the means should never include some alteration of the truth as we know it in Christ. The problem should be regarded as pastoral, and I wonder if its proper liturgical expression should not be found in the Sacrament of Confession.[13]

On the other hand, this more active form of vertical revision tends not to go down well with the older, more traditional believers in almost any denomination. Most Christians seem to sense that there is something seriously out of order if someone is distressed or grieved by addressing God as "Our Father," and they do not look kindly on efforts to alter that address. Consequently, vertical revision of liturgical language risks alienating the rank and file in the nave, those very Christians who pay the parochial and diocesan bills, including the expenses of the liturgical revisions themselves. It is no wonder, then, that those ecclesiastical jurisdictions sympathetic to extreme vertical revision are currently bleeding from every wound. They are in pronounced and rapid decline.[14]

MODIFIED VERTICAL REVISION

Consequently, most Christian leaders, whatever their personal and private views, are afraid to alienate the many traditionalists out in the pews. So they are not disposed to encourage that radical kind of revision. More acceptable to them is what we may call soft, or modified, vertical revision. In this second kind of vertical revision, there is no attempt to introduce feminine names or "balancing" metaphors. Rather, one simply endeavors to avoid mentioning God in masculine words whenever this is possible. Inasmuch as many people pay little close attention to the precise wording of prayers anyway, the revisionists can often get away with it. Thus, the traditional response "It is right to give him thanks and praise" easily becomes "It is right to give our thanks and praise," and not one parishioner in a hundred will notice. Similarly, the majestic "through him, with him, and in him" at the end of the Latin Canon now walks on stilts as "through Christ, with Christ, and in Christ" in Eucharistic Prayer D of the *1979 Book of Common Prayer*. The offending masculine pronoun is avoided. Never, one suspects, have folks been so nervous about pronouns.

But not pronouns alone. This soft vertical revision is touchy about certain nouns as well. In the Episcopalians' *1987 Liturgical Texts for Evaluation*,[15] for instance, "blessed is he that comes in the name of the Lord" is purged of its masculine bias and becomes

190

APPENDIX

"blessed is the one who comes in the name of our God." Thus, both a pronoun and a noun bite the dust. In the same volume, the traditional "the grace of our Lord Jesus Christ and the love of the God the Father" from the Liturgy of St. John Chrysostom (expanding on II Corinthians 13:13) is truncated to read "the grace of Jesus Christ and the love of God." Obviously missing here are the affronting nouns "Lord" and "Father." Now, inasmuch as we have it on good authority (Romans 8:15; I Corinthians 12:3; Galatians 4:5f. See also I Corinthians 8:6, etc.!) that the pronouncements "Abba, Father" and "Jesus is Lord" can be made only in the Holy Spirit, the deliberate omission of them may strike one as a bit serious. Anyway, examples could be multiplied *ad infinitum* from recent liturgical revisions.

Once again, however, I have not detected any such tendency among the Orthodox. Even the popularity of certain speculations[16] about the Holy Spirit being the feminine aspect of God, as it were, seems not to have influenced Orthodox translators of liturgical texts. Orthodox believers still speak of the Holy Spirit as "Lord and giver of life" and invoke him as "heavenly King, Comforter."

HORIZONTAL REVISIONS

What are often called horizontal revision of liturgical language are, or at least seem to be, a great deal less radical. They do not directly affect what we say about God. They leave quite intact and unthreatened the Fatherhood of God and the Lordship of Christ. They makes no direct assault on the Kingdom, so to speak. They share, rather, a common preoccupation of politically correct language in the secular sphere. That is to say, they do not affect how we talk of God but how we refer to one another. In particular, they object to using the masculine noun "man" and its corresponding pronouns when speaking of a human being without reference to gender.

Now this kind of linguistic revision is acceptable to more people, because it is perceived to be of only sociological, and not theological, interest. Thus, the devout hymn-singer who would rather perish than address God as "mother" may feel no discomfort at all with that line in the new Episcopalian Hymnal that alters "and I will raise him up on the last day" to "and I will raise them up on the last day," in spite of the violence it does to John 6. Indeed, in the latest hymnal revisions of the Episcopalians, Lutherans, Methodists, and others, changes of this kind run into the hundreds. Virtually no great hymnographer has escaped being touched up here and there by political correctness—not Joseph Addison, not Charles Wesley, not Isaac Watts.

If the Orthodox in this country should show themselves sympathetic to linguistic revision in their liturgical texts, it will doubtless be in what is called the horizontal mode. Indeed, it is already beginning to happen. There appears to be a rather large number of Orthodox who see no problem in this respect. "Humankind"[17] has replaced "mankind" so

extensively in publications and on campuses that even some Orthodox Christians, especially those deceived by what passes for a college education these days, just take it for granted
that that's the proper way to go.

If you get enough college-educated individuals sufficiently indoctrinated to believe that
"mankind" is sexist, anyone who doesn't tag along can be dismissed as an obscurantist.
This is but a standard instance of what happens when thinking loses its critical edge: an
arbitrary and grandly unexamined hypothesis is unobtrusively raised to a theory, and the
theory is then inadvertently elevated to an *a priori*. Thus, unless subjected to critical analysis (a skill rarely taught in college, I'm afraid), a mere and untried conjecture can be transformed, almost overnight, into a major truth and a self-evident principle.

For example, at the Pittsburgh Convention of the Antiochian Orthodox Archdiocese in
1993, one of my fellow priests insisted that "man" in English, because it is masculine, is
inappropriate as a designation of human beings in general. He preferred the clumsy
"human" as a way of avoiding it. Heaven knows where he picked up the notion.
I refrained from saying so at the time, but he did not know what was talking about.
"Human" is cut from the same etymological cloth as "man." This is obvious if one pro-
nounces "human" with the accent on the last syllable, human, which undoubtedly was the
way it was originally pronounced.[18] To imagine for one moment that to move from "man"
to "human" is to move from a masculine word to a non-gender specific word is possible
only to someone rather ignorant of the history of English morphology.

Both words, "man" and "human," are derived from the Latin *humanus* (yes, with the
accent on the second syllable, hu-*man*-us), the adjectival cognate of *homo*, which is masculine in form and generic in meaning. Thus, both the noun "man" and the adjective "human"
are radically (that is to say, with reference to their root) masculine in form and generic in
meaning. One of these days our feminist thought police are going to discover this fact and
begin insisting that we get rid of the word "human," too. (Unfortunately, if current trends
prevail, the Orthodox translation commission will go along with them.) Since the English
language does not possess a radically non-masculine word for human beings, we will have
to make up one. Perhaps we could call ourselves clabberjugs or monscrandels or something like that.

I did not raise this morphological point with the priest in question. I might have, if he
himself spoke better English. Evidently born abroad, he handled it as a second language
and seemed not at all familiar with it as an object of serious study. He waxed dogmatic on
the subject, nonetheless. I could hardly think what to make of this; even after 30 years of
speaking French and almost 40 years of reading it, I cannot imagine myself arguing about
French usage with an educated Frenchman.[19] On the basis of some half-baked theory,

APPENDIX

however, he was willing to lay abusive hands on something that he showed no signs of understanding. That is the attitude of a vandal. Had I assumed such liberties with his native Arabic, he would have been justly outraged.

POLITICALLY CORRECT

Before tackling specifically the problem of horizontal liturgical revision, such as evidenced in our SCOBA working draft, it will useful to discuss the more general phenomenon of politically correct language, to which the liturgical question is only an extension. I will restrict this discussion to the word *man*, along with its corresponding pronouns, as a designation of human beings in general. There are two points particularly to be made in this regard. First, that it is an entirely correct usage. Second, that the deliberate alteration of this usage must inevitably run against the rock of Christology.

First, the use of the words *man, mankind*, etc. to designate human beings in general is completely and unequivocally proper. It will suffice simply to observe where the accent is placed in the word *humanity*. The contrary thesis, the theory that a masculine noun cannot not be used generically to include women, is only that; it is pure theory, an unrooted conjecture, a fanciful speculation in vogue in that rare, detached atmosphere of bureaucratic, academic America.

Now on this matter, linguistic tradition itself is abundantly clear. Those who contend that the masculine character of "man" is an argument against its generic application must consider that the usage in question is not peculiar to English. Myself, I am no great linguist; I read only a dozen or so languages and have some familiarity with just a few more. But even from this modest exposure I can think of several examples of masculine words normally designating human beings as such, but some of which may, in certain contexts, refer specifically to the male of the species: *ha'adam* in Hebrew, *ho anthropos* in Greek, *'nôshô'* in Syriac,[20] *al-insan* in Arabic, *chelovyek* in Russian,[21] *der Mensch* in German,[22] *de man* in Dutch, *zmogùs* in Lithuanian, *homo* in Latin, along with its multiple derivatives throughout the history of Italian, Spanish, Portuguese, and French.

Even though they normally refer to human beings without respect to sexual distinction, it must be stressed that all of the above instances are masculine nouns, as evidenced by the fact that they take the masculine article when it's available, are modified by masculine adjectives,[23] are referred to by masculine pronouns, and employed with masculine verb forms when the language has them (as in Hebrew and Syriac).

APPENDIX

AN IMPORTANT DISTINCTION

The notion that a masculine noun is inappropriate for reference to human beings in general is a very recent and very weird fantasy. It is solely ideological, not linguistic. So someone who wants to make that argument should be warned in advance that he won't find a shred of support for his case in linguistic studies. In fact, however, our theorists seem not to know much of linguistic studies.

For example, they seem to know nothing about the distinction that scholars make between marked and unmarked uses of nouns. This is very strange, because millions of non-scholars appear to understand the subject quite well. My own babies, for instance, were in full command of it by least age two. The distinction means this: An unmarked noun has two potential meanings: (1) a universal meaning embracing a whole class; (2) a particular reference to something that can be distinguished within the class.

For example, take the unmarked noun *duck*. This word normally refers to all ducks, as in the expression "ducks and geese." In a given context, however, it may refer only to certain ducks. Thus, if I say "one duck and two ducklings," the word *duck* refers only to the adult duck. Its reference is contextualized and thus changed by its juxtaposition to the marked noun *duckling*. The same thing holds with cats and kittens, dogs and pups, pigs and piglets, and so forth. I have yet to meet an English-speaking non-theorist who did not implicitly understand the distinction between marked and unmarked nouns long before he ever started to school.

Contrasts in gender can work the same way. Thus, *fox* when used in conjunction with *wolf* refers to all foxes as a class, in distinction to wolves as a class. When, however, the word *fox* is juxtaposed with *vixen*, it refers only to the male fox. A *dog* can be any dog unless it is juxtaposed with *bitch*; then it means the male canine as distinct from the female. So, too, there are *lion* and *lioness, tiger* and *tigress*, etc. *Fox, dog, lion* and *tiger* are unmarked nouns; they refer to their entire respective species unless properly contextualized to limit their reference.

Nor need an unmarked noun invariably be masculine. So, if I say "geese and ducks," the word *geese* means the whole class as distinct from ducks; but if I say "geese and ganders," the word *geese* moves to its more restrictive reference, which in this instance is the female of the species. In all such cases the context determines the reference. Apparently one forgets something so elementary only when he is sidetracked by a sociology instructor or gets appointed to a translation commission.

Nor is this gender-marking of nouns restricted to English. In fact, the pattern is nearly

194

APPENDIX

universal and can be traced back over four thousand years to our earliest written language, Sumerian. For example, in Sumerian the unmarked noun *dumu* normally means "child," without respect to sex, but it changes its meaning to "son" when it appears in context with *dumu-munus*, "daughter."[24] This is a very early instance of an unmarked noun's simple shift to a contextualized meaning. One will search Pritchard's monumental collection[25] in vain for any evidence that Sumerian women objected to this.

Similarly, in Hebrew *adam* normally means "man" without distinction of sex, but not when employed in juxtaposition to *woman*. In that case it refers specifically to the male; thus, Genesis 2:25: *ha'adam w'ishato*, "the man and his wife." If Grandmother Eve was troubled by this wording, the Bible failed to record it.

The English word *man* is an unmarked noun. Unless its context determines otherwise, it includes any member of the human race. That is its first and elementary meaning, as it always has been. But if I place that same word beside its corresponding marked noun, *woman*, the new context restricts the meaning of *man* to the human male. There is nothing new here. Those who don't know this much about the English language have no business serving on a translation commission.

So, when we profess that God became incarnate "for us men and for our salvation," no rational person under the sun, male or female, can honestly claim that the word *men* is being used in a sense that excludes women. No sane human being has ever truly thought so. The context does not permit such an understanding, and there is something awfully perverse in pretending otherwise. By leaving out the word *men* from that line of the Creed, our liturgical revisers were perversely engaging in that pretense.

OPPRESSIVE LANGUAGE?

Literally thousands of examples from many languages could be cited to show that we are dealing here with a virtually universal phenomenon. It has nothing to do with a distinction between inclusive or exclusive language, because that distinction is political, not linguistic.

Only English, as far as I can tell, among all the languages of the earth, is being subjected to such wholesale political corruption. Nor is there anything quiet or subtle about it, in either method or motivation. Those interested in remaking English vocabulary make no secret of their contention that our inherited tongue, reflecting centuries of deliberate subjugation of women, is inherently onerous, and they endeavor to revise the language as part of a more general reform of society and the political order. Our English language is male-

APPENDIX

dominant to the core, it is argued, and its vocabulary and idiomatic forms must constantly be reassessed with a view to equalizing the sociopolitical advantages of men and women, reversing the antifeminine bias of countless generations.

For example, when the male-affirming, female oppressing word *firemen* can be changed to *firefighters*, then women can be hired for a job hitherto closed to them, and another bastion of male dominance bites the dust. The word *fireman* is seen as an oppressive stereotype manifestly formed with the intention that women be kept from the ranks of firefighters. The very word *fireman* reflects a condescending view of women. How so? Well, they say, it betrays a masculine prejudice designed to keep women in their place (preferably barefoot and pregnant). Men, it is argued, have a very low opinion of women's skills in the face of danger. They fancy that females, in the presence of danger, react irrationally. These men are so insulting as to call this reaction "hysteria," which comes from the same Greek root as "uterus." (What further need have we of witnesses? Their own speech 'betrayeth' them.) These hopelessly chauvinist men patronize women, you see, and treat them as soft, cuddly, easily threatened, and fairly helpless creatures, quite unsuited to the truly significant ventures, the exciting masculine and macho activities, like fighting fires.

Our attention is constantly being drawn to such burdensome stereotypes all through the English tongue, and we are warned that every one of them must be expunged if women are truly to be equal and free. That chiliastic day will dawn only when we stop using words like *man* and *mankind* to designate the human race. Why shouldn't there be a non gender word to designate people in general, so that women are no longer spoken of a sort of subheading of men? English must be remade as part of the re-making of society.

Well, let me state my own response right out: This is drivel. Of course language can be used oppressively, but to claim so deep and radical an oppression against the female, inherent in the very formation of a language, is unlikely on its very face. It is an extreme, unwarranted application of the Sapir-Whorf Hypothesis beyond supporting evidence. It is an indulgence in consummate fatuity that a dozen consecutive seconds of critical reason would suffice to disperse. Even if we must learn new words to do so, we may cultivate any number of personal predilections and prejudices without even slightly altering either the structure of our grammar or the general content of our vocabulary. I may announce, for example, that I hate ants and love spiders, but that would make my language itself neither misomyrmic nor arachnephilic. Similarly, I do not have to master some specialized draconphobic vocabulary to say that I'm scared of dragons, nor need I study the obscure intricacies of gynocentric construction to proclaim that my wife is the center of my life. There are oppressive words in any language, of course, but the object of their oppression is determined by the direction and use of the word, not by a grammatical structure inherent in the language.

APPENDIX

The history of languages does not support even slightly the current notion of an inclusive or exclusive usage. When the Psalmist asked, "What is man that thou art mindful of him," there is not a person alive who honestly thinks that *man* in that context refers only to the male of the species.[26] Likewise, a man-eating shark has also been known to eat a woman (inadvertently?) when the occasion presented itself. On the other hand, the word *men* inscribed on a bathroom door is set in a context that easily permits our distinguishing it from its meaning in, say, the expression "the tongues of men and of angels." Similarly, the word "poet," unless otherwise contextualized, has always been understood to include the "poetess," and so forth *ad nauseam*. It is very distressing to be obliged to insist on something that everybody already knows, but our revisionists will have it so.

Why is all this so hard to grasp? The reason, surely, has to do with a socio political dogma of the academic and elitist thought police, not the noble study of languages, at least not the real living languages spoken by ordinary people uninhibited by feminist and other aberrant ideologies.[27] My illiterate grandmother understood a living language, and so does my very literate daughter. Both of them would find ridiculous the idea that the traditional English language was somehow formulated to oppress them and therefore needed to be changed. My deceased grandmother is unavailable for comment, but my daughter's reaction to the SCOBA draft is a pronounced "yuck."[28]

In short, we are dealing here with a political, not a linguistic, problem, and I am one of those persuaded that socio political questions should be addressed solely on their merits in the light of metaphysical and religious considerations, not by arbitrarily altering the language of the discussion to determine its outcome. The latter approach amounts to poisoning the well just before you drink from it. Those who argue for an "inclusive" language and against an "exclusive" language have no linguistic case to make; solely on the basis of a secular social theory, a political ideology, they are concocting an imaginative distinction, on the unsound basis of which they then proceed to "reform" a precious cultural inheritance. They are vandals laying waste what they do not understand, and even in the secular sphere they should be resisted without quarter, caucus, or compromise. Most emphatically, and for God's sake, we must not incorporate their cultural vandalism into the Divine Liturgy and the Nicene Creed!

LINGUISTIC ENGINEERING

A bit harder to deal with are those who argue that the word *man*, though it originally referred to human beings as such, no longer does so. Those who make this argument claim that current usage limits its reference to the male, while we Neanderthals who stand by the older, traditional, literary meaning of the word are accused of ignoring the march of time and the living, changing texture of vibrant, spoken English.

APPENDIX

This too is rubbish; the very opposite is the case. We are not dealing here with the living evolution by which the meaning of words is gradually altered by popular use. On the contrary, we are being presented with an unnatural and arbitrary fossilization, the fixing of a living thing into the cramped confines of a restricting theory. The current shift in the sense of "man," by which it is applied solely to the male, has nothing to do with a normal development of a vital tongue. It is the witches' brew of a broom-flying intelligentsia. It is caldroned in the midst of strange, circling dancers like the National Organization of Women, The American Federation of Teachers, The American Academy of Religion, The National Educational Association[29] and The Association of Theological Schools, that dark organization that accredits seminaries (and covens).

I am no champion of archaic forms. I am emphatically not advocating either the adoption or retention of old words that have lost their meaning in currently understood English. When expressions do lose or change their significance in the course of living use, then we very well may be obliged to make the necessary adaptations likewise in the vocabulary of our worship. Thus, if the word "man" had actually evolved simply into a marked noun — that is to say: if, in the course of its ordinary and generally understood use among the populace at large, "man" had come to signify only the male of the human species, to the exclusion of the female— then we would have quite a different situation.

That is not, however, the case. It is in the actual spoken English of ordinary people that "man," when not grammatically or socially contextualized, still refers to human beings generally. In the everyday speech of normal citizens who have not been indoctrinated or brainwashed into a specific political ideology foisted on them by elitist thought police, *man* is still an unmarked noun, as it has been from the dawn of our English language.

It is the academics, the political activists, and the feminist-controlled academic publishing industry who object to using the word in its inherited, normal and generic sense. It is invariably the case that those persons who feel uncomfortable using the words *man* and *mankind* in that sense have been made to feel uncomfortable. There are battalions of self-appointed theorists, "experts," and political agitators running around issuing orders these days, especially on the campuses and at the publishing houses. These wardens of the mind keep insisting that we Americans change the way we speak on various matters. Well, they have not made their case. They have simply insinuated their views in contexts where they appear to be authorities, either as teachers, writers, or "experts."[30]

I have watched a generation of college and seminary students forced to adopt this new way of talking and writing. Meanwhile, some of their professors have been denied tenure for not doing so. If academic writers express themselves otherwise, their manuscripts are either rejected or edited to bring them into conformity with the new rules.[31] Such extensive, all-pervasive ideological control of the printing industry seems to me unparalleled in our history. That a writer must reflect a particular social ideology in his very choice of words, or else not get published, certainly justifies my references to "thought police."

APPENDIX

There is an absolute tyranny of the mind going on these days, and if there is one place where the writ of such tyranny ought not to run, that place is the Church of God. Inasmuch as SCOBA's translation commission has attempted to introduce the influence of that destructive ideological tyranny into the Church—indeed, has even submitted the Nicene Creed itself, and specifically the expression of our faith in the Incarnation, to its oppressive strictures—they are forcing us to bow before a secular ideology, and the people of the Church have every right to feel offended.

We are dealing here with what Robert Sokolowski called "an iconoclasm of language." Commenting on certain changes in liturgical language being proposed in the Roman Catholic Church (and now adopted by our own Orthodox liturgical commission!), he wrote of "engineered changes" being recommended for the language of worship, among which he numbered the alteration of the word *man*. He remarked that these engineered changes serve as noise or static, they are intrusive, they shout and proclaim a point of view, inserted by certain people between the believer and God, between the believer and the message of faith. No one is responsible for the traditional forms of English, but a definite group and a definite point of view are expressing themselves in the engineered forms. They are imposing their will on others.[32]

When I raised this same question with one of the members of SCOBA's translation commission, he assured me that absolutely no member of that commission could justly be accused of sympathy with a feminist philosophy. Doubtless he was right. I am not accusing them of such a thing. I am saying, rather, that their adoption of a politically correct "human" in place of the traditional "man" was manifestly inspired by a desire to conform to the current but unjustified dogma of the campus and the academic publishing industry. That dogma does not represent either traditional or popular English. It is ideologically driven, and the major driving force is a vandalistic feminism. If in charity we acquit our SCOBA translators of evil intent, we must still deal with this lamentable fruit of their manifest naiveté and historical myopia.

THEORY AND TRADITION

This is but another instance of a current battle between the democratic aspiration of a living tradition and the conjectural concoctions of an academic elite. Since most people are naturally reluctant to change, these theorists must usually resort to political pressures brought to bear at certain advantageous points and catch the other side off-balance. I observed elsewhere:

The academic world, the domain of books and laboratories that sometimes seems to exist solely for the cultivation of experiment and theory, most often is such a point. Make no mistake. The theorist really does have the theories. That is to say, he is an idea man and is at home on the campus and at the publishing house. He does his homework. He has thought the thing through and worked it out. The bugle then summons him forth from the library. His well-marshaled arguments bristle in their serried ranks; his eager footnotes snort and paw the ground.[33]

Today's theorists have grabbed hold of the campus and most of the publishing industry. Nobody nowadays, not even Abraham Lincoln were he still among us, could say in a classroom, or publish in a book, anything even faintly resembling "our fathers brought forth" without losing his job, getting a call from the censor, or being sued for sexual harassment.

I learned something of this struggle a few years ago, prior to coming to the True Faith. I was serving on the faculty of Trinity Episcopal School for Ministry, in Pennsylvania, during the period when it was seeking accreditation from the Association of Theological Schools (ATS). Those sent to interview us as part of the process were the most ideologically invasive men I have ever met. At every point, even with regard to such matters as the financial policies of the school, we found ourselves facing the arrogance of arbitrary dogmatic presuppositions from which there was scarcely an appeal. At the end of the whole unpleasant experience of multiple interviews with these swaggering, self-important dogmatists, from which I conceived a fierce hatred of everything they stood for, one of my *confreres* remarked that at last we had found the reason for the colossal decline of theological studies in the United States.

In particular, this nefarious group made strenuous efforts to impose a stern ideological control over the language patterns of our faculty's lectures in ways neither subtle nor free from threat. In the end only our equally unsubtle invocation of "academic freedom" caused the scoundrels to back off. It was instructive that these armed investigators from ATS could respond sympathetically solely to another elitist theory; appeals to common democratic decency were of no avail. Two years ago, when I published an article describing this experience, an Orthodox bishop wrote to thank me for it, remarking with some consternation that ATS is also the accrediting agency of our own Orthodox seminaries, including his alma mater!

While I am referring to the struggles of that Episcopal seminary against the invasion of secular ideology, I may remark in passing on an incident that occurred there in 1989, just after I left. The priestess that the seminary unwisely hired that year to teach pastoral theology promptly issued a directive to her students containing her required guidelines for tests and term papers. Such papers must not, she told them, use "man" or "he," etc., when referring to human persons, and so on. Well, there was still some vestigial sanity in the place in those days, so the faculty, honoring a sincere and monumental uproar of the student body,

APPENDIX

obliged the priestess-professor to rescind the directive. I wonder if this incident will return to haunt them when time rolls around for the renewal of their accreditation by ATS.

Now let me suggest strongly that the Orthodox Church must not concur in this elitist disposition to alter the mother tongue for purposes of ideological tyranny and social engineering. Indeed, the Orthodox Church should fiercely resist it. The deliberate corruption of a people's inherited, living language is a point at which the prophetic invective of the Church is appropriately directed. At the very least, the Church must not cooperate with this iconoclasm, this concerted, wanton vandalism of a noble tongue with a view to the political control of thought.

CHRISTOLOGY

A final incident from my Episcopalian days may serve to illustrate my next point. At the seminary chapel on Ash Wednesday one year I was placing blessed ashes on the heads of those few seminarians who did not consider the rite excessively "catholic." As I did so, I pronounced each time the ancient and sobering admonition that traditionally went with those ashes: "Remember, man, that thou art dust, and unto dust shalt thou return." Everything was moving along fine until I suddenly was accosted by one of our female seminarians, who said: "Please, don't call me *man*." Well, I didn't. And the loss, I am persuaded, was hers.

The symbolic thrust of that Ash Wednesday rite, as I understand it, is repentance, an essential component of which is the confession that in Adam we all die. Eve was an *adam* too, of course, being human; she was formed from her husband's rib and thereby shared his own nature. Still, Adam was the head of the race, not Eve. St. Paul does not say that "in Eve all die" (cf. I Corinthians 15:22). Not that Eve was not a sinner, for certainly she was (cf. II Corinthians 11:3; I Timothy 2:14). But precisely because she was not the male, not the head (cf. I Corinthians 11:3; Ephesians 5:23), the fall of our race is specifically ascribed to Adam, not Eve. If every human being is a sinner, it is because "in Adam all die." It was the male who bore the very name of our race. It was Adam who transmitted to us the fallen condition, the demonic bondage, these humanly desperate circumstances that render our repentance necessary.

I have already indicated that our SCOBA translators were ineluctably doomed to fail in their search for a non masculine word for human beings. If they are ever to accomplish the eradication of even the least trace, the faintest flavor, of masculinity when speaking of the human race, they will doubtless have to invent an entirely new tongue.

But also an entirely new theology! Our vertical and horizontal linguistic references cross, you see, at a specific point: Christ. He, I submit, is ultimately the reason why the

APPENDIX

horizontal revision of liturgical language is just as invalid as the vertical. By reason of the Incarnation, God looks at the world through human eyes. The horizontal and vertical lines are joined in the Cross. In Christ those two linguistic references, divine and human, while remaining distinct, nonetheless stand in a hypostatic union at a specific point, and the endeavor to treat them separately amounts to a kind of linguistic Nestorianism.

They are seriously deceived who imagine that the ideological manipulation involved in deliberate linguistic engineering has nothing to do with Christian theology. Let us be clear on this point: Anything we do to anything human touches Christ, and this principle applies also to that foundation of all culture our speech. Whatever we do unto even the least of our nouns, we do unto him. This current experiment in radical social restructuring by the ideological regulation of language is grievously offensive, then, not only to man, but also to God, who has hypostatically entered our race.

Because of Christ, the old Adam is no longer the head of humanity: "As in Adam all die, so in Christ shall all be made to live" (I Corinthians 15:22). As death reigned in all men because of Adam's disobedience, so righteousness and the energies of God's very life begin to reign in those incorporated into Christ (cf. Romans 5:14-21). He is the true Head (Ephesians 1:22; 4:15; Colossians 1:18; 2:19). My worry for the young lady who would not be called "man" was deadly serious, the adverb being understood here theologically. How in the world could she come to life in Christ, if she disassociated herself from death in Adam?

Consequently, it is theologically significant, and not just a happenstance of grammar, that the nouns for "human being," in the languages I surveyed earlier, are uniformly masculine. According to Christian theology, headship among human beings abides properly in the male, a truth independently adumbrated, as it were, in the anatomies of those languages. All of the human race, including the first woman, comes from Adam, the original head and source. Christ is our new Head. The masculine form of the divine assumption of our human nature in the Incarnation was not an accident of biology. The male-ness, the masculinity, of Christ is not peripheral to the mystery of salvation.

Obviously our recent translators were attempting to find a word for human being that was not masculine. As I explained above, they failed because their preferred word, *human*, is of exactly the same root etymology as *man*. The deeper reason why they failed, however, is more than mere morphology. Futile as it was from a grammatical perspective, it was also not good doctrine. It was a flouting of theology as well as grammar.

Those who fancy that horizontal linguistic revisions are all right so long as we don't engage in vertical revisions are kidding themselves, for in Christ those two things meet and remained fixed forever. A good example of such self-delusion, as I write this in late

APPENDIX

September of 1995, is the Most Reverend Donald W. Trautman, the Roman Catholic Bishop of Erie and the chairman of the Roman Catholic bishops' committee on liturgical translations. Long a partisan dedicated to "moderate" horizontal linguistic revision, Bishop Trautman professes to be deeply shocked by the new inclusive language version of the Bible published by Oxford University Press.[34] Poor man, he is horrified that the biblical "Son of Man" has suddenly become "the human one" at the hands of liberal Protestant translators, while the Lord's Prayer is now addressed to "Our Father-Mother in heaven." And, pray tell, why not?

Because man is made in God's image and likeness—and most especially because of that divine assumption of our nature by which the Son, for us men and for our salvation, became man—everything human is theological. To impose any of this current nonsense on humanity is to impose it on Christ, and to impose this nonsense on Christ is to impose it on God.

The moment even the slightest credit or validity is conceded to an ideologically driven, politically correct canon of secular social theory, one is giving away the whole game. As soon as someone starts reciting 2, 4, 6, 8, 10, he may stop, for we already know what the rest of the numbers are going to be. He who says A, B, C, will eventually get around to R, S, T. In the integrity of a living language, as in biology, it is impossible to be a "little bit" pregnant. Those churchmen who toy around with these secular doctrines, whether in liturgical translations or by planning workshops at our seminaries, are showing themselves awfully naive. However unintentional, I have no doubt of their threatening great havoc to the Church.

HIERATIC LANGUAGE

A second serious difficulty of this new translation is its almost complete abandonment of hieratic forms. I take this latter category to include those words and expressions that have come, by custom and in the course of time, to be restricted to certain sacred contexts, such as the Bible and worship, and not normally in use outside of those contexts. This category embraces such words as *thou, thee,* etc., along with the corresponding verb forms *dost, canst,* and such verbs as *vouchsafe* and *beseech* and so on.

Let me say at once that my objection to this abandonment of traditional hieratic vocabulary and grammar will sound somewhat muted, if compared to what I said above about politically correct language. Privileged to serve the Divine Liturgy at a local Romanian monastery each week, I rarely hear the nuns use that hieratic language in their chants, and I can't say for sure that I miss it very much. On the other hand, I always use it at the altar, nor do the sisters seem to mind.

Since most of my daily prayer is not said in English anyway and hasn't been for many

APPENDIX

years, I admit to not having strong personal feelings on this matter. I recognize, nonetheless, that very many people do, and I wonder why the commission thought it necessary to insist on this perfectly arbitrary alteration that is sure to bother a great number of people in the Church. That number includes, I believe, every single member of my own parish! Some of them have been singing "and with thy spirit" for upwards of eighty years, and now along comes some SCOBA commission with its narrow, little prejudice and tells them that they must not do that anymore. Nor will the response be different among the young. The teenagers in my parish will likewise think the whole thing junk.[35]

Why go interfering unnecessarily with the way people pray? If their prayer is not in heresy, if it has been nourishing their souls for decades, even if it is composed in a hieratic tongue, alien in some particulars to their everyday speech but still perfectly intelligible at every point—then, why not just back off and leave those people alone?

Just where was the mandate for all this blue nosing? The commission was supposed to work out some reasonable adjustment of the various translations so that the different jurisdictions would be using pretty much the same words. It was never generally understood, I think, that they had such a free hand to go ideologically messing around with a people's accustomed habits of worship. Unless it is absolutely imperative to change the way people pray, it is disturbing, divisive, and destructive to do so. Our revisers may, therefore, learn first hand that Baumstark's Law[36] is a real law, with very real sanctions.

Even more than the laity, however, this change from hieratic language is going to hit the priests of the OCA and the Antiochian Archdiocese. Most of the instances of that special vocabulary are found in the priest's parts of the service, those blessed words dear to the priestly heart and around which a priest does well to build his whole life. Indeed, very often (though not in my own case, usually) these prayers are recited *sotta voce*, inaudible to the congregation. In other words, only God and the priest will hear them anyway. (Some priests don't even use English for them.) If we are talking about words that are whispered quietly by lips accustomed to praying them devoutly for years, why on earth step in and arbitrarily intrude a bias on them?

I suggest what I believe to be a workable solution. Is conformity so necessary? Or is even consistency within a given translation really indispensable? Inasmuch as congregations of the Greek Archdiocese have not been using these hieratic elements for the past decade, we should not, I think, make them obligatory. There is no need to make Greek Christians pray in a way to which they are not now accustomed. Is it not possible to find room for both usages, to be determined locally and on the basis of pastoral consideration?

After all, even the translation commission stopped short of altering the hieratic style of

APPENDIX

the Lord's Prayer, recognizing that there are limits beyond which it is pastorally unwise to disturb people. Now, if it is all right for Orthodox Christians to say "thy kingdom come," why not let them say "and with thy spirit"? If it is acceptable to use such words as "hallowed be thy name," surely there could be nothing out of place also to say "save thy people and bless thine inheritance." Why be so rigid about this?

STYLE

This new translation is flatter than a pancake. There is no *élan*, no melody, no disciplined cadence. It escapes being dry and dull only at those points where it is merely awkward. It stops imitating CNN now and then, only long enough to simulate Barnum and Bailey. Scarcely any attention seems to have been given to considerations of sonority, such as the placing of accents, the varying lengths of alternating vowels, and the sequential flow of consonants. Is it not remarkable that the Liturgy of St. John Chrysostom, the richest and most elaborate ritual in Christendom, should be accompanied by such a stale English style?

Neither space nor time will permit my listing every example, but let me cite a couple by contrasting them to their material equivalents in Bishop Basil's translation.

Observe how a stately clause can be cut off at the knees by a crude shift of accent and the sudden loss of alliteration. This is exactly what happens to Bishop Basil's "no one who is bound with the desires and pleasures of the flesh" when the commission abruptly throws it into a half-nelson: "no one bound by worldly desires and pleasures." Leaving aside, if we must, the fact that the earlier translation is certainly more faithful to the underlying Greek (*sarkikais*), what about the mere sound of the thing? The rhythm of the earlier rendition is balanced by a sonorous construction of long and short vowels, the integrated pairing of two "esh" words ("pleasures of the flesh"), and the force of the final accent on a monosyllable. Every single melodic feature of this fine, flowing line disappears in the later version, which has no fluidity and is governed by no cadence.[37]

Again, note what happens when an ideological bias forces the translation from a "thou" to a "you." Bishop Basil's translation reads: "Holy art thou, and all-holy." Except for the soft, unobtrusive *t*, *th* and *d* sounds, the entire phrase is pronounced near the back of the throat, with a chiastic arrangement of the dominant vowels: roughly *o-ah-a-ah-o*. Not one component is formed by the lips. The resulting timbre is a sustained *ah*, if you will, expressive of rapture, wonder, and adoration.

Now what of this is left in the new version? Well, check for yourself: "Holy are you and

APPENDIX

most holy." Whoever is responsible for this pitiful line knows precious little about English.[38] The clumsy construction "holy are you" is not only alien to the tradition of liturgical English but is simply a weird way of talking in any context. But leave aside that common-sense assessment. Simply note what happened to the earlier sustained *ah* sound of the phrase noted above. It's gone. The timbre has now been shifted to the front of the mouth by the intrusion of oo ("you") and "most." The carefully crafted sonority of wonder and adoration disappears. The sensation of rapture is gone. The entire experience is different. Style, here, is not simply style.

The SCOBA commission's working draft is bothersome in a multitude of other particulars of style. I give one more example brought to my attention by Archbishop Dimitri of Dallas: hitherto, we among the Antiochians and the OCA have long been accustomed to singing, several times during the Divine Liturgy, "let us commend ourselves and each other and all our life". The new rendition, following the Greek usage since 1985, has changed "commend" to "commit." I hate to sound picky, but that does not work. While either word can be justified as an adequate translation of the underlying parathometha, they are not otherwise equal. "Commit" fails on two points in particular. As Archbishop Dimitri remarked, "Just how can I commit another person? I can commend someone else, but I can commit only myself." Well put, I think. In addition, there is a matter of sonority. The short *e* of "commend" is vastly more singable than the short *i* of "commit," and the line is normally chanted. In sum, the reasons for this dubious alteration are well shy of obvious.

PRAYER STRUCTURE

I particularly object to the SCOBA working draft's disposition to change invocations into plain affirmations. I must begin by explaining what I mean by this.

A very traditional structure of prayer is an invocation followed by a petition. Its simplest form, perhaps, contains just two words: "*Kyrie* (invocation), *eleison* (petition)." These can be expanded in various ways that lengthen the prayer without disturbing its underlying structure. Thus "Kyrie" becomes "Lord, Jesus "Christ, Son of the Living God", and "eleison" is augmented to "have mercy on me a sinner." The prayer is thus lengthened and becomes more contemplative. The traditional Jesus Prayer is just a slightly longer meditation on the Kyrie eleison. Literally hundreds of liturgical prayers are structured exactly like this.

Thus, there is the expanded invocation: "O heavenly King, the Comforter, the Spirit of Truth, who art everywhere present and fillest all things." That is simply an unfolding, if you will, of "Kyrie," except that it is addressed to the Holy Spirit. And how do we dilate the "eleison"? "Come and abide in us and" so forth. The Divine Liturgy's initial calling

APPENDIX

upon the Holy Spirit is just an expansion of the "Kyrie eleison."

Try this example—The invocation (Kyrie) is:
O Lord our God, whose might is beyond compare, whose glory is incomprehensible, whose mercy is boundless, and whose love toward mankind ineffable—That invocation is then followed by the petition (eleison): look down upon us and upon this holy house, and grant us and those who pray with us thy rich mercies and compassion.

This same structure of the collect is just as well known in the West. For example, examine this expanded invocation: "O God, who art the author of peace and lover of concord, in knowledge of whom standeth our eternal life, whose service is perfect freedom." This is followed by the augmented petition: "defend us, thy humble servants, in all assaults of our enemies, that we, surely trusting in thy defense, may not fear the power of any adversaries." All we have here is a longer version of the "Kyrie, eleison." I do not exaggerate when I say that I would have no trouble filling this entire essay with identical examples of this structure from liturgical texts east and west over the past 2000 years: from St. John Chrysostom, from St. Leo the Great, from Archbishop Cranmer and so forth.

The invocation part of such prayers can expanded in a variety of ways: adjectives ("all-holy, good, and life-giving"), titles in apposition ("O Existing One, Master, Lord, almighty and adorable Father"), relative clauses ("who hast bestowed on us these common and united supplications," "who hast appointed in heaven orders and hosts of angels," "who art hymned by the Seraphim") and so forth. Literally hundreds of them begin with variations of "Almighty and everliving God who ..." Now in the newer translations, beginning with the Roman Catholics 30+ years ago, this "who" is gone. Those components that originally followed it are no longer part of the invocation itself, but have been transformed into declaratory sentences beginning "you." The one who prays is not invoking; he is declaring. Thus, I am no longer calling at length upon the name of the Lord; I am, rather, somewhat artlessly entrusting him with information about himself. This shift alters the entire tone of the prayer. Style here, once again, is not simply style. We are talking about the movement of the soul in speaking to God.

Our older Orthodox translations generally respected that traditional structure.[39] Not this new one. Following the lamentable model of the Roman Catholic efforts, our components of invocation are changed to declaration in dozens of places, disrupting the flow of the prayer. The long, stately sentences of the anaphora, for example, are broken up into choppy pronouncements, not tied together structurally. Reading them, I know that they lose in dignity, but I cannot figure out what in the world they gain. Why are we imitating

APPENDIX

the Roman Catholic versions in one of their worst features?

START OVER

I chanced upon some privately published comments on the SCOBA working draft by Father John Shaw, a Milwaukee priest of the Russian Orthodox Church Outside of Russia. Father Shaw's first objection is that this translation will accomplish the very opposite of its original intention: to further the unity of Orthodox Christians in the United States. He senses—correctly, I have no doubt—that the ideological bias of the commission's work will prove very disruptive and divisive. Far from encouraging unity among us, he suggests it "could be a major source of scandal to anyone raised in the Orthodox tradition."

That assessment, in my opinion, is wonderfully understated. This version will be a scandal also to those of us who were not raised in the Orthodox tradition but fought and clawed our way to the Orthodox Church from out of the jungles of heresy. Its very appearance on the Orthodox scene as a "working draft" is already a source of widespread disappointment and distress, perhaps throughout the whole Church in America.[40] Moreover, at this very moment there are literally hundreds of Protestants and conservative Roman Catholics, in despair of finding any theological stability where they are now, who are looking to Orthodoxy as a possible future home for themselves and their families. I pray a merciful God they do not see this new translation.

Apropos the SCOBA translation project, a wise Orthodox abbess recently remarked to me that it would be irresponsible to adopt any translation that caused widespread dissent and disaffection. Better not to have a new translation at all, she insisted. She is right. This work must not be inflicted on the Church.

FOOTNOTES

[1]On pp. 952, 953, 971, and 984 of the *1979 Book of Common Prayer,* one may note in the daily lectionary that Romans 1:26-27 and I Corinthians 6:9-11 are deliberately omitted from the *lectio continua,* so that Episcopalians would be spared hearing what God thinks of homosexual sin. Hence, although it is not yet listed in the Prayerbook, Aids Awareness Sunday is rapidly becoming a major feast day in the Episcopal Church.

[2]This Service Book, commissioned by St. Tikhon of Moscow and translated by an Anglican, uses the Coverdale Psalter throughout. It has been kept in print by the Antiochian Archdiocese since 1917. For the record, we may note that that Archdiocese also published the first English music books for choirs in the 1920s, and in 1938 one of its priests, Father Seraphim Nassar, produced *The Book of Divine Prayers and Services,* the first—and still today the only—comprehensive collection of texts needed for the chanting of complete services in English.

[3]"The Challenge of Liturgical Language," *Doxa,* Transfiguration-Dormition 1994, p.1.

[4]Cf. *Didache* 14.3; Justin Martyr, *Dialogue with Trypho* 116.3; Hippolytus, *Commentary on Daniel* 4.35; Irenaeus, *Proof of the Apostolic Preaching* 1.10; Aphraat, *Demonstration* 16.3; Augustine, *Paschal Sermon on the Sacraments* 1; Cyril of Alexandria, *Commentary on Sophoniah* 2.39; *Commentary on Malachi* 1.1; John of Damascus, *The Orthodox Faith* 4.13.

[5]I often serve Divine Liturgy at the Monastery of the Transfiguration, a very edifying house of nuns of the Romanian jurisdiction, where the community provides for my aging eyes with a large-print edition of a translation authorized by Metropolitan Ireney back in 1967 and reprinted by St. Tikhon's in 1977. It is very similar to the present version used in the Antiochian Archdiocese, though not in every respect quite as good.

[6]I hear that this is still happening, by the way, and think it lamentable.

[7]Evidently, archepiscopal authority put a stop to this aberration immediately. Had things gone otherwise, I doubt that I would still be getting nocturnal calls from Episcopal clergymen all over the country, asking how they can get into Orthodoxy. Similarly, last May at the Rose Hill Conference in South Carolina, when Bishop Kallistos (Ware) urged that the Orthodox Church keep an open mind about ordaining women to the priesthood, one of my Episcopal friends remarked that "he lost a bunch of potential converts with that suggestion." (I am planning to comment on this incident in the pages of *Touchstone* in the near future.)

[8]This was the last time I received any work of the commission without specifically asking for it. I am grateful to Father Joseph Fester and Father Edward Hughes for copies of the latest version, on which my present comments are based.

FOOTNOTES

[9]Most, but not all. It relies on the version of the Greek Archdiocese in a majority of instances.

[10]Well known, I think. Under the pastoring hand of Metropolitan Philip, the Archdiocese has grown from 60 or so congregations to 195; 20 ex-Protestant congregations were added shortly before I was chrismated in 1988, and 35 more have been added since, most of them from formerly Anglican parishes; 78% of our present clergy are converts to the Orthodox Church.

[11]Oddly, the revisers must have been napping at the beginning of their labors; the initial "on earth peace, good will among men" somehow managed to elude their ideological vigilance.

[12]Dedicated to the refutation of this idea was an entire issue of *Mission and Ministry* 8/2, Fall 1990.

[13]Patrick Henry Reardon, "Imaging God," *Touchstone* 3/4, 1990, p.16.

[14]The Episcopalians, having lost at least one-third of their membership since ordaining women and vandalizing *The Book of Common Prayer* in the 70s, are the most obvious and distressing example. In November of 1994, to be sure, the chief bookkeeper of the Episcopal Church, Ellen Cooke, reported a modest growth of 12,483 new members, but most people, and certainly most Episcopalians, are now disposed to put scant trust in Mrs. Cooke, a circumstance arising, one suspects, from her admitted embezzlement of $2.2 million in church funds. This latter tragedy adds yet another burden to a seriously demoralized denomination already bent over double by the accumulated weight of heresy in its seminaries, scandals among its clergy, published allegations of impropriety in the management of its pension fund, the loss of whole congregations, and rampant feminist and homosexual politics, all of this topped off by the arrogance, drivel, and moral imbecility of the worst presiding bishop in its history. Recent, sobering analyses of the state of the Episcopal Church include Dale D. Coleman, "A Stubborn Presiding Bishop," *The Living Church*, July 30, 1995, pp.8f.; William Murchison, "Last Rites," *National Review*, July 31, 1995, pp.55f.; the anonymous editorial "No Joy in Mudville," Foundations, July -August 1995, pp.4-6; David Mills, "A Hope of Collapsing Churches," *Touchstone* 8/3, 1995, pp.17-23; Doug LeBlanc, "Gay Bishop Urges Integrity: 'Light a Candle' Under SLC [Standing Liturgical Commission]," *United Voice* 8/1 September 1995, p.4; David W. Virtue, "Church Pension Fund Gambles With Episcopal Clergy's Future," ibid., pp.1,5-8.

[15]Published by the Standing Liturgical Commission of the Episcopal Church, this text was sent to all Episcopal seminaries for trial use. Pennsylvania's Trinity Episcopal School for

210

FOOTNOTES

Ministry, where I was Old Testament professor at the time, was one of these, but after carefully studying the volume the faculty voted unanimously not to use it. Under the able leadership of the Dean, the Very Rev. John Rodgers, we were the only seminary in the Episcopal Church to take that stand.

[16]In my opinion, unfounded and dangerous speculations, even if they are associated with some big names.

[17]Strictly speaking, however, I think "human kind" is better written as two words. That usage is both logical (inasmuch as "human" is an adjective) and traditional (cf., for example, Samuel Johnson's Rambler column of October 13, 1750, in The British Essayists, London: Woodfall, 1823, Volume 16, p.331).

[18]Thus says the Oxford English Dictionary and what I think to be the consensus of scholarship.

[19]Neither can I imagine myself serving on a commission to make a French translation! It has been suggested that membership on such translation commissions should normally be restricted to those who speak the terminal language as their mother tongue. After all, it is argued, we are not talking about translation into illiterate languages, as so many of our Orthodox forebears have accomplished, starting with Sts. Cyril and Methodius. English is a highly complex, nuanced language with centuries of vast literature, including a rich deposit of liturgical and devotional literature. Knowing this, the earlier Orthodox translators into English wisely sought help from those more familiar with that deposit. Still, there is no need to be apodictic in this respect, I think. Native-born Americans are every bit as capable of ruining a good liturgy on their own, nor am I aware of any evidence that the sad results of our commission's labor can be particularly ascribed to those members whose native language is other than English.

[20]It is curious, though, that the Peshitta sometimes uses the specifically male *gabra'* to translate the Greek *anthropos*. John 19:5 is an example.

[21]Russian, Lithuanian, and Latin do not have articles.

[22]The cognation of this noun to the English *man* is more obvious if one puts the latter into plural, *men*. German further distinguishes *der Mann*, the human male, from the pronoun *man*, referring to no person in particular; thus *man sagt*, "one says," in the sense that "it is said."

FOOTNOTES

[23]In a period of over 2000 years of Greek literature, I know of only two or three instances where *anthropos* is modified by a feminine adjective, and the contexts of those show that they referred to specific women.

[24]Paul V. Mankowski, S. J., "A Fig Leaf for the Creed," *Touchstone* 7/2, Spring 1994, p.11-14.

[25]*ANAT*, or *Ancient Near Eastern Texts Relating to the Old Testament*, Princeton University Press, 1969.

[26]The Hebrew here uses the more poetic '*enosh*, following it with the parallelism *ben adam*, "son of man." (The latter expression, manifestly masculine, nonetheless includes women too. The Hebrew Bible never says *bath adam*, "daughter of man," nor have I been able to find it in rabbinical works.) Reading down the columns of the Koehler/Baumgartner Lexicon and Lisowsky's Konkordanz, one see that such fluid constructions are not unusual in the Hebrew Bible, where even a more specifically "male" expression is sometimes used generically when it suits an idiomatic context. That sort of thing seems not to have bothered the inspired Psalmist, but it draws the very brain waves out of his recent feminist translators. Cf. Patrick Henry Reardon, "Christology and the Psalter," *Touchstone*, 7/2, Spring 1994, pp.7-10.

[27]Living literature is also based on popular language, not on the jargonese of the ideological elite. Were he writing today, I am confident that Hemingway would not entitle his novel *The Senior Citizen and the Sea*.

[28]Incidentally, she is no dumbbell, and I have high hopes of her getting through college without being brainwashed. She is currently doing a double major in German and French at Duquesne University, if I may be pardoned this reference to someone of whom I am inordinately proud.

[29]This is the group that declared October "Gay/Lesbian History Month," calling on school districts and teachers to plan month long observances with displays, films, and guest speakers to enhance appreciation of homosexual culture among children from K to 12.

[30]Two years ago, when I first objected to the direction taken by SCOBA's translation commission, that same fellow priest reminded me reproachfully that the commission was composed of "experts," whom I was unqualified to challenge.

[31]This appears to be true even of formerly conservative publishing houses like Eerdmans and InterVarsity.

FOOTNOTES

[32]Robert Sokolowski, "Splitting the Faithful," *Crisis*, March 1993, pp. 24-27.

[33]Patrick Henry Reardon, "Theory and Tradition," *Touchstone* 6/4, p.25

[34]I rely here on a report from the Catholic News Service published in Louisville's *The Record* 117/38, September 21, 1995.

[35]Those who imagine that young people will feel more drawn to worship if it is done in "street English" may want to check out the disappointing results of that experiment among the Roman Catholics and Episcopalians during the past three decades.

[36]Roughly, and from memory, it says that the more primitive forms are more probably preserved on the more solemn occasions.

[37]It is identical here to the Holy Cross translation, by the way. One has the impression that the latter served, at least implicitly, as the model for the SCOBA draft. That's too bad, because the Holy Cross version was by far the worst one up the present time.

[38]It appears, however, to have no composer but only to represent a stupid compromise among differing members of the commission. My evidence for this assessment comes from the Holy Cross version which has the rather pedestrian "You are holy and most holy."

[39]A lamentable exception is found in the Russian version reprinted by St. Tikhon's in 1977, which begins its first collect with "O Lord our God, Thy power." Fortunately, it redeems itself by the third collect: "O Thou who hast given us grace."

[40]I have spoken mostly with local Greek and Russian clergy, every one of whom expressed dismay and disappointment about it.